CHRIS RISER

WHAT IS LOVE?

*Understanding & Demonstrating
Biblical Love*

What is Love?
Understanding and Demonstrating Biblical Love
By Chris Riser

Scripture taken from the New American Standard Bible, @1960, 1962, 1963, 1971, 1972, 1973, 1975, 1977, 1995 by The Lockman Foundation.
Used by permission.

Cover Design by Jessica Mohr.
Interior Design: Jennie Lyne@bookpageit.com

ISBN 979-8-9867186-2-0
eBook 979-8-9867186-3-7

Printed in the United States of America.

Published by:

Maryville, TN
www.gracemaryville.org

To my children—Josiah & Emily, Johanna, Selena, & Marie – for the joy of the love we have so richly shared.

Thank you to Chrismole Abraham, Debbie Bate, Linda Davis, Yvonne Hanson, Ronald Martin, and Rachel Slate for reading early drafts and providing feedback.

Special thanks to the Grace Community Church elders for modeling the love spoken of in this book and to Jessica Mohr for prompting, directing, and shepherding forward every aspect of this book.

And He said to him, "'YOU SHALL LOVE THE LORD YOUR GOD WITH ALL YOUR HEART, AND WITH ALL YOUR SOUL, AND WITH ALL YOUR MIND.' *This is the great and foremost commandment. The second is like it,* 'YOU SHALL LOVE YOUR NEIGHBOR AS YOURSELF.' *On these two commandments depend the whole Law and the Prophets.*"

~ Matthew 22:37–40 ~

———————————————

7

CONTENTS

Introduction 1

Chapter 1 5

   Drop Anchor 7

   I Want to Know What Love Is 8

   The Greatest Commandment 9

Chapter 2 13

   A Time to Love and a Time to Hate 14

   One Further Question, Your Honor 18

Chapter 3 21

   Hear, O Israel! 23

   How Do I Love Thee? Let Me Count the Ways . .24

   An Object Lesson 24

   The How-to's of Love 26

Chapter 4 . . . . **29**

Love Is Supernatural 30

Love Is More Than an Emotion 31

Love Is More Than a Verb. 32

Love Is More Than Sacrifice and Obedience 34

Love Is Relational. 35

Love Is Selfless and Humble 36

Love Is Not Based on Merit. 37

Love Is Christian and Desires the Highest Good.38

Love Finds Full Satisfaction in God. 39

Infinite Love for Eternity 40

Chapter 5 . . . . **41**

Love Is Defined by Scripture 42

A Defining Moment 44

Chapter 6 . . . . **51**

Second Best 53

Love Thyself? 56

Perception Correction. 59

A Warning for Warmth 60

Chapter 7 63

Won't You Be My Neighbor? 63

Another Defining Moment 67

Content is King 68

Chapter 8 71

Summing It Up, Breaking It Down 72

Love is Supernatural 73

Love Is Relational 74

Love Is Selfless and Humble 77

Love Is Obedient to Scripture 78

Chapter 9 81

The Greater Good 82

Love is Helping Others Look like Jesus 83

Come What May 85

You Love Me and I'll Love You 86

Jesus, Lover of My Soul 88

Copycat Love. 89

Effective Love 90

Chapter 10 93

A Tuesday to Remember. .93

Love Fulfills the Law 95

An Unpayable Debt 96

Love Motivates and Empowers 98

Love In Deed 99

Chapter 11 103

The Blessing of Christ 104

The Blessing of the Spirit 105

The Blessing of the Word 106

The Blessing of the Church 108

Questions for Reflection. 111

INTRODUCTION

Love is the Mount Everest of Christian virtues. For a Christian to properly reflect the character of God in Christ, he must express the love of God which has been shed abroad in his heart by the Holy Spirit (Rom. 5:5). The love of God is the subject of the most well-known verse in the Bible: "For God so loved the world, that He gave His only begotten Son, that whoever believes in Him shall not perish, but have eternal life" (John 3:16). The greatest commandment is to "LOVE THE LORD YOUR GOD WITH ALL YOUR HEART, AND WITH ALL YOUR SOUL, AND WITH ALL YOUR MIND," and the second is like it: "YOU SHALL LOVE YOUR NEIGHBOR AS YOURSELF" (Matt. 22:37, 39). Love motivates obedience, fuels the fear of the Lord, and anchors human relationships. Yet for all its emphasis and importance, love remains one of the most misunderstood words in the Christian vocabulary.

Given the fact that the world is infatuated with love and completely unable to understand or exercise it biblically, this is not surprising. Every secular love song and every new Disney movie continues to perpetuate stereotypes of love which, at their very best, are merely echoes of the real thing. Unfortunately, the Christian world has imbibed the spirit of the age in this regard and tends to mimic the same concepts of love that the world holds dear, such as: love is in the eye of the beholder (i.e. *whatever I want you to do for me is "love"*); love is from the heart (i.e. *whatever arises from my heart is the way to express love*); and love is a blind emotion that cannot be helped (i.e. *whatever my emotions and desires drive me to do is acceptable in the name of love*).

Scriptural love, on the other hand, expresses love that is defined biblically (i.e. *whatever God want me to do is love*), comes from a heart transformed by the Holy Spirit (1 John 4:19), and is an informed motivation, directed through knowledge and discernment.

However, even stronger, more Biblical views can still fall short of the totality that Scripture describes love to be. When asked about love, many quote 1 Corinthians 13: "love is patient, love is kind" (vv. 4–8), etc. But without a proper understanding of love as a motivation empowered by the Holy Spirit, these expressions of what love does can be co-opted by nearly any religion or humanist movement. Certainly, true love "does" all the things described in 1 Corinthians 13, but to be truly Christian, *these actions must be motivated by the glory of God in Christ.*

Even the concept of self-sacrifice for the good of others—often the definition given by theologians—is not a sufficient description of biblical love. In the same passage to the Corinthians, Paul stated that one can give all his possessions to feed the poor and even deliver his body to be burned—all without love (1 Cor. 13:1–3).

Perhaps the most controversial proposition of this book is that despite what might be called the "echoes" of love found in society—deeds of human kindness, warmth of affection, extreme acts of sacrifice—only Christians can *truly* love. That is, only those who have been born of God have the necessary resources to love as God loves.

The meaning of love matters. If we misunderstand its definition, we will live the Christian life with little strength and effectiveness. We will lose the true power of love and suffer from a watered-down substitute.

Thus, my purpose in this book is to reexamine the biblical passages on love—specifically focusing on Christ's response to the Pharisees in Matthew 22:37–40—to draw out the motivation that drives love, the power that enables love, and the purpose for which love is exercised. When these truths are properly understood, we are able to pursue love in a truly biblical way and properly reflect the character of the God who *is* love.

My prayer is that as you read this book, you will be challenged and comforted by the radical nature of God's love for you. As a result, you will be able to love others more deeply and more biblically, thus truly fulfilling God's first and second commandments with joy and effectiveness.

C. R.

CHAPTER 1

A powerful river current has just swept you away. Enveloped by foamy, churning rapids, you gasp for air, anxiously searching for anything on which to grab hold. Your eyes finally land on a tall patch of reeds jutting out into the water. You strain every fiber in your body to reach for the ends of those thin shoots. As you clutch your fist around a handful, they snap like blades of grass. The flimsy stalks prove utterly useless to save you.

Such a scenario inspired the expression "grasping at straws,"[1] meaning that failure is pretty much a foregone conclusion. Like bringing a toothpick to a gunfight, it's essentially pointless. That's how it is when the world tries to define love. They are undertaking a task of equal futility:

---

1 John Prime, *A Fruitefull and Briefe Discourse in Two Bookes* (London: Thomas Vautrollier, 1583), 30. Full text is accessible through the University of Michigan, https://quod.lib.umich.edu/e/eebo2/A10112.0001.001/1:4?rgn=div1;view=fulltext. A similar phrase was used also by Sir Thomas More, *Dialogue of Comfort against Tribulation* (1534): "A man in peril of drowning catchest whatsoever cometh next to hand . . . be it never so simple a stick."

- "*Love* is blind."

- "I'm falling head over heels in *love*."

- "If you *love* something, set it free."

- "Real *love* means never having to say you're sorry."

- "*Love* makes the world go round."

- "I'm hopelessly in *love*."

- "I'm blindsided by *love*."

- "It was *love* at first sight."

Syrupy platitudes like these are everywhere in our society. The world is desperately lost when it comes to the true meaning of love. Everybody wants it. Everybody is searching for it. Yet nobody seems to actually understand it. The inherent difficulty of pinning down the notion of love has in no way dampened attempts.

But the world is grasping at straws.

One straw may proclaim self-care: "You can't love others until you love yourself first." Another may offer no judgment: "Love is love—that's all that matters." Yet each thin reed buckles under scrutiny. Pastor Mike Riccardi succinctly summarizes the problem as follows:

> [T]he wisdom of secular society has failed to define love biblically. To our self-indulgent, narcissistic, perennially adolescent, self-willed culture, "love" means nothing more than [psychologist] Carl Rogers' notion of unconditional positive regard. To "love" someone, according to our society, is to affirm every decision they make and to applaud them just for being them. Bruno Mars' hit song is the soundtrack to Western secularism's gospel of

unconditional acceptance: "You're amazing, just
the way you are."

. . . [P]eople have confused the idea of being
affirmed, accepted, flattered, and made much of
with true love. Loving me means making me feel
good by making much of me. And this ideology
of love . . . is woven into the fabric of our cultural
consciousness. To believe anything else would be
un-American.[2]

Even the church at large appears to grapple with what love
truly is. Influenced by the culture around them, Christians
schizophrenically cobble together a contradictory patchwork of
man's wisdom and God's wisdom.

Rather than surrendering their own preconceptions
to the authority of God's Word and seeking to
understand how God defines love, they use their
own distorted definition of love that they have
imbibed from our society, and they foist that
definition onto the Scriptures and onto their
conception of God.[3]

This straw breaks in two. At best, it's not helpful, and at worst,
it affirms as loving what the Bible deems to be hateful.

Drop Anchor

God, however, has graciously provided an anchor on which to
cling—His holy Word. Unlike the papery straws, this anchor is
immovable and never fails. If we want to understand love, *it cannot
be found or understood apart from the character of God and the person
and work of Jesus Christ as revealed in His Word.* Any so-called

---

2   Mike Riccardi, "Love, Hate, and Homosexuality," *The Cripplegate*, August
3, 2012, https://thecripplegate.com/love-hate-and-homosexuality/.
3   Riccardi, "Love."

love not based on Scripture and empowered by the Holy Spirit is a crude counterfeit that offers no eternal benefit. *Jesus Himself is the model for, and the foundation of, the love that forms the central motivation for all relationship and obedience in the Christian life.* If we really want to understand love, we look to Jesus. But I'm getting ahead of myself.

I Want to Know What Love Is

The Bible has many things to say about love. The apostle John taught that "God is love" (1 John 4:8). He stated that "everyone who loves is born of God and knows God" (4:7). Jesus bucked tradition by instructing His hearers to sincerely love their enemies (Matt. 5:44). God provides an account of joyful, marital love in Song of Solomon. He also gives an example of honorable love as displayed by Boaz in the protection of his future wife, Ruth.

The overarching theme throughout God's Word, though, is *His redemptive love.* If you grew up in church, you no doubt heard this verse: "For *God so loved the world*, that He gave His only begotten Son, that whoever believes in Him shall not perish, but have eternal life" (John 3:16, emphasis added). The perfect, holy God who created the entire universe ordained a way for sinful men to come into His eternal presence. Marred by our corrupted nature inherited from disobedient Adam, our attempts to be sufficiently righteous are like, well, grasping at straws.

In fact, John Prime, the sixteenth-century English pastor who originated the saying, was discussing this topic when coining the expression. Describing sinful man's efforts to procure a righteous standing before God, Prime said he "catch[es] at every straw" on his way to judgment—*if and until* he "appeals to the throne of grace" and lays hold of "His endless favour and everlasting mercy."[4]

Christians in no way earn their right standing before God but wholly rely on Christ's perfect righteousness instead. Our

---

4 Prime, *Discourse*, 30.

good works following salvation flow out of a Spirit-indwelt heart
that longs to express gratitude to God through obedience: "For
this is the love of God, that we keep His commandments; and
His commandments are not burdensome" (1 John 5:3). We love
Him, and we love to obey His commands. Psalm 119 declares:

> I shall give thanks to You with uprightness of heart,
> When I learn Your righteous judgments.
> I shall keep Your statutes. (vv. 7–8)
> With all my heart I have sought You;
> Do not let me wander from Your commandments.
> Your word I have treasured in my heart,
> That I may not sin against You. (vv. 10–11)
> I shall delight in Your statutes;
> I shall not forget Your word. (v. 16)
> I shall delight in Your commandments,
> Which I love. (v. 47)
> O how I love Your law!
> It is my meditation all the day. (v. 97)

In fact, loving God *is* itself a commandment! And not just
any commandment, but *the* commandment.

The Greatest Commandment

Beginning the end of His earthly ministry, Jesus set His face like
flint toward Jerusalem (Luke 9:51). His essential mission of bearing
the Father's wrath for our sins unto death still lay ahead of Him. He
and His disciples joined the other Jews pilgrimaging to Jerusalem
for Passover week. The shouts of "Hosanna in the highest!" that
greeted Him at His Triumphal Entry would quickly be replaced
by calls to "Crucify Him!" by the week's end.

At the beginning of the observance, though, Jesus ministered
in the temple before the crowds. Devising plans to get rid of Him,
the whole cadre of Israelite elites showed up to entrap the Son of

God. Like a gang of goons lining up to unsuccessfully combat the flying limbs of Bruce Lee, the chief priests, Pharisees, Scribes, other elders, Herodians, and Sadducees all took their shots at Christ— one by one, but to no avail. With perfect ease, He handily repelled every scheme intended to rout Him. Like the great martial artist, He even redirected their attacks back on them.

They challenged His authority, but Jesus responded with parables that unmistakably accused them of rejecting their Messiah. He promised judgment for refusing to rightly recognize Him as God. Incensed, they persisted in peppering Him with loaded questions in hopes He would implicate Himself. Instead, He masterfully exposed their hypocrisy and so-called self-righteousness.

In one instance, Christ wrested victory from the Sadducees who tried to stump Him with a hypothetical question about marital status in the resurrection. At this point, Jesus was already batting a thousand, and the crowds were astonished (Matt. 22:33). Scripture records, "[W]hen the Pharisees heard that Jesus had silenced the Sadducees, they gathered themselves together."

Before Jesus launched into a full-throated condemnation of the scribes and Pharisees, they brought in the heavy artillery—a Pharisaic lawyer (*double whammy!*)—for one final question. They were emboldened to make one last attempt to discredit Jesus. Despite their losing record, they persevered because publicly vilifying Him was the first step in the larger plot to kill Him. In their minds, much was at stake.

The lawyer asked Jesus, "[W]hich is the great commandment in the Law?" (Matt. 22:36). In other words, what is the single, most critical commandment to follow? What is of chief importance? Around what should we structure our lives? Spoiler alert: Jesus gives the perfect answer. (Does that surprise you?) The answer, in short, is *love.*

Since love is what this little book is about, we're going to dive deeply into Jesus' answer. If this is the one thing we need to nail down, then we must fully understand it. We must plumb the depths of what love truly is, so we can practice it—and thereby obey, honor, worship, and glorify our Lord.

Jesus' answer to the lawyer will not only cover our relationship with God but with every single person. As with any time we encounter the truth of God's Word, we should come away changed. Prepare to be impacted by understanding what biblical love actually is. The subtitle of this book, though, is not just "understanding" love but "demonstrating" it. Are we truly loving God and others? What does that look like? How do we love people we don't even know, or worse, who've greatly harmed us? We are not simply gaining knowledge, although it must start there. We will learn how to apply it in our lives.

Thankfully, we have His Word. As already stated, the Bible is not a mere straw to be grasped, but a steadfast anchor on which to cling. Let us prayerfully consider and heed the words of our Lord and Savior.

CHAPTER 2

In the summer of 1914, an Austro-Hungarian prince and his wife traveled down to an annexed territory to attend a routine military exercise. Some nationalists there resented the empire's takeover. In fact, a cabal of underground revolutionaries conspired to assassinate the emperor's heir. Aware of the danger, the prince and his entourage proceeded anyway, even parading down the capital's main avenue in an open-topped vehicle.

Though a handful of the young colluders lost their resolve, one brazenly hurled a bomb directly at the prince's automobile, only to have it bounce off the folded rooftop and roll under another car in the procession. Surprisingly, the explosion did not cause the prince to immediately flee the city. Finishing the planned itinerary, he even swung by the hospital to visit the officers wounded by the bomb.

As the motorcade eventually whisked them out of town, they mistakenly turned onto a side street where one of the handful of conspirators just happened to be standing. Before the driver could rectify the error, the enraged nineteen-year-old pulled out his pistol and shot both the prince and his wife. Within minutes, both were dead, and within weeks, the entire world was at war.

The assassination of Archduke Franz Ferdinand lit a powder keg of complex alliances, causing the First World War to break out across the globe.[1]

A Time to Love and a Time to Hate

The Pharisees had an assassination plot of their own. The move to publicly trap Jesus in His own words (to later use against Him) was just a piece of that larger plan. They were ruthlessly determined to bring about His death because He had become their ultimate nemesis. He threatened their political power, religious authority, social status, and all the money, prestige, freedoms, moral superiority, clout, luxuries, respect, and security bound up in their positions.

The Pharisees, therefore, were not simply gluttons for punishment who enjoyed losing these verbal battles with Christ; they formed this unholy huddle before their final question because everything that meant anything to them was at stake.

In one sense, they were right. Jesus did come to upend our lives. For those who follow Him, He expects a willingness to leave "houses or brothers or sisters or father or mother or children or farms for [His] name's sake" (Matt. 19:29). He declared, "If anyone wishes to come after Me, he must deny himself, and take up his cross daily and follow Me" (Luke 9:23). The Pharisees should have recognized Christ's deity and their utter lack of holiness in light of His character, but their arrogant love for themselves prevented such a response.

Before we advance to their closing question, do you, dear reader, comprehend the cost of bending the knee to Christ as Lord? That it means you—your life, your desires, your hopes, your rule, your authority—are completely relinquished? That is the precise price to follow Him. So often in the world of cultural Christianity,

---

1 Jesse Greenspan, "The Assassination of Archduke Franz Ferdinand," History. com, June 26, 2014 (updated February 12, 2020), https://www.history.com/news/the-assassination-of-archduke-franz-ferdinand.

though, a thin coat of Christ is painted onto our own pursuits in life. He is framed to fit our desires, yielding a man-centered view focused on *Him* serving *us*. We can't have our cake and eat it too. He is mutually exclusive.

Jesus made clear the cost is high—but the reward is invaluable. He explained, "For whoever wishes to save his life will lose it, but whoever loses his life for My sake, he is the one who will save it" (Luke 9:24). While He takes from us, He gives back infinitely more (and better).

Sadly, the Pharisees refused to believe in Him. While Jesus' followers were coming empty-handed as required, the Pharisees' hands were so crammed full of their own self-righteousness and all the worldly acclaim it brought, they could not and would not release their grip.

Before Christ even started His earthly ministry, John the Baptist preached repentance and baptized those who "confessed their sins" (Matt. 3:6). When the Pharisees and Sadducees came to John to be baptized themselves, John exclaimed: "You brood of vipers, who warned you to flee from the wrath to come? . . . [D]o not suppose that you can say to yourselves, 'We have Abraham for our father'; for I say to you that from these stones God is able to raise up children to Abraham" (3:7, 9). Their proud hearts merely wanted to add another notch on their religious belts. In just a few words, John stripped away their claims of distinction and inherent goodness.

Jesus, likewise, exposed the Pharisees for their hypocrisy throughout His ministry, but they were in for the excoriation of a lifetime after this Q & A session ended in the temple that day. Jumping ahead for a moment, here's just a sampling of it:

> But woe to you, scribes and Pharisees, hypocrites, because you shut off the kingdom of heaven from people; for you do not enter in yourselves, nor do you allow those who are entering to go in. . . .

Woe to you, scribes and Pharisees, hypocrites! For you tithe mint and dill and cummin, and have neglected the weightier provisions of the law: justice and mercy and faithfulness; but these are the things you should have done without neglecting the others. You blind guides, who strain out a gnat and swallow a camel!

Woe to you, scribes and Pharisees, hypocrites! For you clean the outside of the cup and of the dish, but inside they are full of robbery and self-indulgence. You blind Pharisee, first clean the inside of the cup and of the dish, so that the outside of it may become clean also.

Woe to you, scribes and Pharisees, hypocrites! For you are like whitewashed tombs which on the outside appear beautiful, but inside they are full of dead men's bones and all uncleanness. So you, too, outwardly appear righteous to men, but inwardly you are full of hypocrisy and lawlessness.

You serpents, you brood of vipers, how will you escape the sentence of hell? (Matt. 23:13, 23–28, 33)

You can probably imagine their response. The boiling hatred that resulted from such a public censure only fueled the murderous intent already festering in their wicked hearts.

The person and work of Christ is intrinsically offensive to the world. The world hates Him and His followers. Why are we sometimes surprised by the derision of our faith when Scripture literally warns us to "not be surprised" by it (1 Pet. 4:12)? We may hope that somehow the world will embrace us with open arms, but as our culture continues to darken and shake off the quasi-Christian vestiges from our societal roots, the real, antagonistic response to Christ is more evident. As we witness the truths and principles of Scripture coming under attack, we must not be fooled into thinking we could ever be friends with the world.

The radical commitment that Christ requires of us brooks no compromise. Jesus gave plenty of heads up:

> If the world hates you, you know that it has hated Me before it hated you. If you were of the world, the world would love its own; but because you are not of the world, but I chose you out of the world, because of this the world hates you. Remember the word that I said to you, 'A slave is not greater than his master.' If they persecuted Me, they will also persecute you; . . . all these things they will do to you for My name's sake, because they do not know the One who sent Me. . . . He who hates Me hates My Father also. (John 15:18–21, 23)

In fact, if the unbelieving world loves being around you, examine yourself. That's not a good sign. Jesus was letting us know that we should expect to be treated like He was. This has often been the case throughout history and is happening even now around the world. Led by the Pharisees, the world gathered against Christ; and the world will continue to gather against those who love Him.

Peter informs us that our "adversary, the devil, prowls around like a roaring lion, seeking someone to devour" (1 Pet. 5:8). He sought to devour Christ, and believers are no less in his sights. Consequently, we must be "of sober spirit" and "on the alert" (5:7), remembering that "the whole world lies in the power of the evil one" (1 John 5:19). He and his minions stoke the flames of the world's hatred. They give no quarter. Nothing must be surrendered to them.

Jesus endured these attacks that were quickly escalating and would soon culminate in His murder.

One Further Question, Your Honor

On February 8, 1982, off-duty police officer Raymond Hubbard was shopping at a local mall in Maryland when he witnessed a jewelry heist in progress. He bravely intervened but was tragically shot to death by the robbers. While three accomplices were convicted and sentenced, a fourth man was tried the following year. Harlow Brian Sails vehemently denied the charges, insisting his alibi proved he could not have committed the crime.

Coupled with conflicting eye-witness testimony, reasonable doubt was looking more certain in his court case—that is, until the prosecuting lawyer Arthur A. Marshall, Jr., cross-examined him on the witness stand. With each question, the attorney took the wind out of Sails' sails. As his story began to crumble, Sails shocked the entire courtroom by dropping the charade and confessing to murder: "[G]asps of surprise rippled through the courtroom," according to the *Washington Post*, as Marshall successfully incriminated Sails.[2]

The Pharisees aspired to the same success—that Jesus would slip-up and publicly say something worthy of capital punishment. They would even settle for something slightly foolish or controversial to twist out of context and flip the consensus of public opinion against Him. The huddle broke and the heavy hitter stepped up: "One of them, a lawyer, asked Him a question, testing Him" (Matt. 22:35). This was not spontaneous. They planned for this expert to interrogate Jesus.

A lawyer in Jesus' day, however, is not quite the same as what we think of today. This lawyer would have been an expert not in human law, but the law of God—the Mosaic law. Though for the Jews, these two were indistinguishable. They were essentially the same.

---

2   Sandra R. Gregg and Leon Winter, "Murder Defendant Recants Story, Admits Shooting," *The Washington Post*, January 8, 1983, https://www. washingtonpost.com/archive/local/1983/01/08/murder-defendant-recants-story-admits-shooting/c3adbb46-70ab-4060-b207-e04a01377fef/.

He would have been considered a specialist in the interpretation and application of the law. If someone had a question about the law, they would summon this guy. He would consult his collection of the Scriptures, examine the additional commentaries and traditions the religious leaders added throughout the intertestamental period, and render an answer.

Many years ago, my church hosted a youth camp in Amish country. The kids got a firsthand look at the Amish religion that is based on a legalistic system not unlike the Pharisees'. While famously shunning electricity, they do allow their adherents to ride bicycles. Even then, the rubber comprising the tires must meet a certain threshold of rigidity; otherwise, a softer tire may provide too much comfort. They did this with *everything*. At one point, we asked our Amish tour guide how they determine all these little rules. Without hesitating, he responded, "Oh, there's a council."

Any question that arose—like the degree of softness in bicycle tires—was determined by the council. Like the lawyer, they would study the established traditions and their gnarled interpretations of scriptural principles and provide a decision to be respected.

The Pharisees used the lawyer's legal acumen to craft the best possible question that would most likely capture a response upon which they could bring accusations. The parallel passage in Mark describes the lawyer as truly impressed with Jesus' earlier answers, but this in no way lessens the overall motive of the Pharisees (Mark 12:28). They were determined to find grounds to condemn Him.

We finally arrive back at our question introduced in chapter 1. The lawyer asked of Christ, "Teacher, which is the great commandment in the Law?" (Matt. 22:36). With that, the query dropped, the crowds fell silent, the "Teacher"—who is also Messiah, Master, Lord, and King—didn't miss a beat, sharing what this one thing is.

In the next chapter, we will begin to examine Jesus' response. Prepare your own heart if you find anything lurking that smacks of the Pharisees' attitude. Consider Jesus' warning that His followers must be willing to deny themselves. Be ready to carefully receive His words as truth.

CHAPTER 3

When Jeanne Louise Calment celebrated her birthday in 1995, she made international headlines. What made the French woman's birthday so special was her 120th time observing it. When someone asked what kind of future she expected, she wryly quipped, "A very short one."[1] She was right. When she died in 1997 at 122 years of age, she set the record for the oldest person in modern history. Aside from genetics, researchers attributed Calment's long life to exercise and low stress—hardly surprising. In fact, a study of a group of centenarians revealed that their "secrets" to longevity included active lifestyles, mental exercise, moderation in eating, reduced stress levels, and a positive outlook on life.[2] Pretty straightforward—makes you wonder why they needed researchers in the first place.

We concluded the last chapter with the final question that the Pharisees posed to Jesus. They wanted to hear from Him

1   Craig R. Whitney, "In France, A Citizen Turns 120," *New York Times*, February 22, 1995, https://www.nytimes.com/1995/02/22/world/in-france-a-citizen-turns-120.html.
2   Alexa Mellardo, "Longevity Secrets of the Oldest People in the World," *Eat This, Not That!* March 16, 2022, https://www.eatthis.com/news-longevity-secrets-oldest-people/.

what He thought the greatest commandment was. Much like the predictable geriatric study, Jesus gave a straightforward, even somewhat expected, answer:

> And He said to him, "'YOU SHALL LOVE THE LORD WITH YOUR GOD WITH ALL YOUR HEART, AND WITH ALL YOUR SOUL, AND WITH ALL YOUR MIND.' This is the great and foremost commandment. The second is like it, 'YOU SHALL LOVE YOUR NEIGHBOR AS YOURSELF.' On these two commandments depend the whole Law and the Prophets." (Matt. 22:37–40)

Jesus had already answered the same question before on several occasions. He had nothing new to say. In Luke 10, yet another lawyer had already stood up to test Jesus. The law expert asked a similar question: "Teacher, what shall I do to inherit eternal life?" (v. 25). Instead of answering, Jesus turned the question back on the lawyer, asking him: "What is written in the Law? How does it read to you?" (v. 26). He replied by quoting the same passage Jesus recited in Matthew 22. Jesus affirmed the answer as correct (v. 28).

So, why would the Pharisees pose the question again? While we can't really know for sure, it could be in part due to the large, ongoing debate among contemporary religious leaders at the time. Different schools of thought had different rankings for the top commandments, so perhaps they hoped He would jump into the confused fray and undermine His claims. Or maybe they thought he would introduce some novel line of thinking that would contradict Mosaic law. He had already advanced some radical ideas in their opinion; maybe He would take an antinomian turn and nullify the law altogether if they were lucky.

Hear, O Israel!

Let's begin to dissect Jesus' answer. He quoted a command from the Old Testament that is very familiar to most of us. For them, *familiar* would be an understatement. It would have been the first words for many of the Jews. In fact, it was the most cited passage for the Israelites. They could have quoted it in their sleep backwards and forwards. The Shema (from the Hebrew word for *hear*) is a Jewish prayer taken from Moses' instructions to the Israelites:

> "Hear, O Israel! The LORD is our God, the LORD is one! You shall love the LORD your God with all your heart and with all your soul and with all your might. These words, which I am commanding you today, shall be on your heart. You shall teach them diligently to your sons and shall talk of them when you sit in your house and when you walk by the way and when you lie down and when you rise up. You shall bind them as a sign on your hand and they shall be as frontals on your forehead. You shall write them on the doorposts of your house and on your gates. (Deut. 6:4–9)

The Pharisees would have repeated this prayer when they woke up every morning. Mark's parallel account records Jesus citing verse 4 as well and includes both "mind" and "strength" (Mark 12:29–31). Matthew, meanwhile, only adds "mind" to the original Deuteronomic command. The point does not lie in the manner or number of divisions but in the comprehensive nature of love—more on this in a moment. Essentially, *we are to fully and perfectly love God.*

How Do I Love Thee? Let Me Count the Ways

While "love God" sounds like a simple enough concept, if I asked a hundred different Christians what that meant, I think I would get a hundred different answers. None of the answers may even be unbiblical, but very few of them may be sufficiently all-encompassing and exhaustive. Does it simply mean to emote back to God? To kindle a passion toward Him? Or is it delighting in Him? In serving and obeying Him? Is love a verb? It's all those things but much, much more.

When we fall short in our understanding of what it means to love God, we fall short in everything else. We cannot love others properly, our worship of God is stunted, and our walk with the Lord is harmed. Despite the crucial weight of grasping this concept, many of us just settle for our piecemeal thoughts on the matter.

If I asked another hundred Christians what the greatest commandment is, the vast majority would no doubt answer correctly—just like many of the Pharisees who truly believed they loved God. From self-righteous Pharisees on one end of the spectrum to self-proclaimed libertines who presume upon God's love on the other, the concept of love has been distorted every which way.

With this in mind, let's see if we can't clear up and correct any confusion. We are going to be challenged by the nature, depth, and importance of real love. As believers, we desire to love God with all our hearts, souls, might, minds, and every other part of our existence. By understanding true biblical love, we can properly demonstrate it wisely and well.

An Object Lesson

Walking down an aisle of home décor, you will most likely see trendy pieces that have the words *Believe* or *Faith* written across them. Perhaps you even have some in your home. The world loves these words, too. The culture's vague ideas of belief and faith have no meaning, however, apart from the *object* of that faith and belief. The object means everything. It makes all the difference.

With that said, we must first understand the Object who commands our primary love—"the LORD your God." The words recorded in Greek correspond to the Hebrew words *Yahweh* (or YHWH) and either *Adonai* or *Elohim*, respectively. This is the great *I AM*, the covenant-keeping, omniscient, omnipotent, sovereign Creator of the universe who graciously and lovingly adopted us into His family.

He is not a god of our own making, suited to fit our own values and broadened and diluted to include all religions. The Object of our affection is not the kindly, old grandpa, nor is He our personal genie or little tribal deity. He is neither the man upstairs who winks at sin nor our co-piloting buddy who can lend a helping hand. He's not the harsh taskmaster or cosmic bully nor the aloof, deistic Designer detached from His creation. He does not evolve with culture, adopting their fashionable causes, nor is He simply a force in the universe exacting karma on mean people. He is the God of the Bible.

What it means to "love the LORD your God," then, is entirely and exclusively defined by Scripture. God Himself defines it by His self-disclosure to us. There is no other God than the God of the Bible. He has revealed Himself to us in the truth of His revelation. Theologian J.I. Packer observed, "To follow the imagination of one's heart in the realm of theology is the way to remain ignorant of God, and to become an idol-worshipper—the idol in this case being a false mental image of God, made by one's own speculation and imagination."[3] So critical it is to ensure we are adoring the true God of the Bible, A.W. Tozer asserted, "What comes into

---

3 J.I. Packer, *Knowing God* (Downers Grove, IL: InterVarsity Press, 2021), 47–48.

our minds when we think about God is the most important thing about us."[4]

The world loves "god" when they create him in their own image—or decide to take him out of existence altogether. Sadly, mainstream evangelicalism is increasingly inventing a god worthy of worship according to societal values. When they are confronted with the objective reality of who God has revealed Himself to be in the Bible, they perform theological gymnastics to avoid exalting that God.

Remember to whom the Pharisees addressed this question: God the Son. In fact, after Jesus answered their question, "while the Pharisees were gathered together" (v. 41), He turned around and asked them, "What do you think about the Christ, whose son is He?" (v. 42). Jesus was going to simultaneously prove that the Messiah was none other than God in the flesh *and* directly expose their full-fledged rejection of Himself as the foretold Savior.

After sharing the most essential commandment with these supposed law-keepers, He unmasked them as the law-breakers they truly were. As Christ explained to His disciples, "He who rejects Me rejects the One who sent Me" (Luke 10:16). They could not profess to love the Father but hate His Son. To love the trinitarian God of the Bible, one must love all three persons: Father, Son, and Holy Spirit.

That last question from Jesus in the exchange was left ringing in their ears, as "[n]o one was able to answer Him a word, nor did anyone dare from that day on to ask Him another question" (Matt. 22:46). Their silence betrayed their outright dismissal of their own promised Deliverer.

The How-to's of Love

WikiHow is one of the top websites for how-to instructions on just about anything. Clicking on their "Random Article" button, one

4 A.W. Tozer, *The Knowledge of the Holy* (New York: HarperCollins, 1978), 1.

can discover: "How to Play Outside Linebacker," "How to Design a Garden," "How to Crack a Whip," "How to Learn to Accept Your Nose," and "How to Raise Quail," among other various skills to add to one's repertoire. Search for "How to Love God" and there's surprisingly a "trusted expert" who has indeed written a step-by-step guide for that as well. Thankfully, we have the Bible not only to know *whom* we are to love, but *how*.

As we mentioned earlier, loving with heart, soul, and mind does not have so much to do with how many parts we can be divided into as with the comprehensive nature of that love from every part of our inner man. What is the inner man? It's everything on the inside that makes you...*you*. God created us both body and soul—we are material and immaterial, physical and spiritual, outer and inner. By *inner man*, I don't mean your pancreas but your soul. The inner person encompasses the mind, will, conscience, emotions, affections, and individual personalities that distinguish us from each other.

The Bible may interchangeably use terms such as *heart, soul, mind*, or *spirit*, but the reference is always to our inner being. While one text may focus on intellect and reason, another may be emphasizing passions and affections. Combined, the inner man is the "seat of man's collective energies, the focus of personal life, the seat of the rational as well as the emotional and volitional elements in human life."[5]

Here in Christ's response, He most likely used *heart* to stress vigorous, sincere effort. Paul had that full exertion in mind when he commanded, "Whatever you do, do your work *heartily*, as for the Lord rather than for men" (Col. 3:23, emphasis added). The use of *soul* may address the will and desire, the very life force of our being. *Mind* points to the intellect—what is known and understood as a rational being. Contrary to the world's idea of love as merely a passion, the mind is a critical component of love. Paul prayed

---

5   George Abbott-Smith, *A Manual Greek Lexicon of the New Testament* (New York: Continuum Books, 1999), 230.

that the Philippians' love would "abound still more and more *in real knowledge and all discernment*" (Phil. 1:9, emphases added).

Altogether, true love means that the heart has been transformed; every piece of it has been devoted to delight in God. We cannot reserve any part of us and withhold it from God. This great commandment is foremost because every other command hangs on it. Obedience to God's moral law is based on a love for Him that marks true Christians. Let's begin to examine this biblical love.

CHAPTER 4

Our church prints and passes out gospel tracts that advertise a "biblical view of salvation." Does that mean we tacitly admit there are other valid views on salvation of which the Bible's perspective is one? Of course not. The implication is that the biblical view is the *correct* view—that is, it rightly corresponds to reality, straight from the Creator of reality Himself. This goes for everything.

You may have heard sermons, podcasts, blogs, or booklets titled as biblical views of sexuality, wealth, government, morality, and much more. Does this mean another point of view is simply being tossed into the ring of ideas? Or perhaps that we believe it's the *best* view? Well, a biblical view *is* the best view, but that's because it's the right view—the only true view. Biblical humility, for example, represents the understanding of humility as it actually exists. A biblical view means God's view, and God possesses the clearest and purest view of reality since He's the One who defines it! Biblical humility, then, is true humility. Biblical morality is true morality, and so on.

That said, as we dive into defining biblical love, keep in mind this means *love* as the Creator of love defines it according to His Word. *Biblical love is true love.* While this love has varying expressions (within marriage or between brethren in Christ, for example), the heart attitudes are still the same. Jesus used the Greek term *agapeo* for this commandment. Unlike the similar brotherly affection of *phileo* love, the natural-flowing, familial attachment of *storge* love, or the fleshly, sensual *eros* love, *agape* love is the Bible's flagship term of choice. So, what does it mean? What is true love?

To seek a comprehensive explanation, we will first examine many distinguishing characteristics of biblical love in general. Then, we will make a division based on the two commandments Christ presented: *love to God* and *love to neighbor*. It's critical to be as precise as possible. Each will have their own separate definition. In fact, not until halfway through the next chapter can we begin to piece together an exhaustive definition for *love to God*.

For now, let's look at biblical love, broadly speaking. Imagine it as a tree. This chapter will begin to examine the main boughs that branch off from the trunk. Then we'll work our way downward to get to the root.

Love Is Supernatural

Our first branch, or aspect, is that real love is fundamentally supernatural—that is, it originates outside of ourselves. Love is empowered by the Holy Spirit because it comes from God. This means *the natural man cannot love in this way.* True love is not a mere human emotion; nor is it even an earthly commitment. The apostle John was clear: "Beloved, let us love one another, for *love is from God*; and *everyone who loves is born of God* and knows God" (1 John 4:7, emphases added). There's no more challenging sentence in the Bible than that: *No unbeliever ever loved biblically a single time—not once.*

Unbelievers can exercise echoes of this love, undoubtedly, but their unregenerate hearts are devoid of the Holy Spirit and remain spiritually dead. They can be the epitome of niceness, even kind, generous, gracious, sacrificial, and patient, but they can never demonstrate *biblical* love because it's supernatural.

Renovating the heart, the Holy Spirit empowers it to love. Apart from those who have been changed by God, no one can exercise biblical love. John continued, "The one who does not love does not know God, for God is love" (1 John 4:8). The world produces reverberations of this love, but it's not the same thing, even though we may use the same word.

Love Is More Than an Emotion

While the world ever increasingly encourages emotions to be the engine driving our behavior, decisions, and direction in life, the Bible puts them in the caboose, the last car of the train. Emotions aren't unbiblical—far from it. God emotes! But our emotions, which are informed by our thinking and marred by our sin, are stubborn. They may not always dutifully fall in line. In short, love can be felt emotionally, but this experience is *not* a requirement for love's exercise or benefit.

Emotions are never a necessity of love. They can often accompany it, but they're not essential. If they were, then we could never truly love until we properly generated enough "loving feeling" toward another. What would that precise feeling even be? This emotional requirement greatly limits and diminishes love. Biblical love is free from the constraints that demand an emotive component always be present.

In reality, I can be loving when I discipline my children, when I confront someone in sin, or even when I persevere through a harrowing trial and *feel* like I'm coming apart at the seams. For believers, whether our emotions may be turbulent or absent, our affections—the deep-seated attachments within our souls' core desires, motivations, and attitudes—are always present and directed Christward. Paul prayed for the hearts of the Ephesians to be strengthened,

> so that Christ may dwell in [their] hearts through faith; and that [they], being rooted and grounded in love, may be able to comprehend with all the saints what is the breadth and length and height and depth, and to know the love of Christ which surpasses knowledge. (Eph. 3:17–19)

Compared to this deep plea of Paul's, attempts to whip up some cheap, saccharine imitation through emotional appeals to the flesh fall woefully short.

Love Is More Than a Verb

Back in the nineties, as contemporary Christian music was growing in popularity, hip-hop trio DC Talk released a song entitled "Luv is a Verb."[1] In it, the rapper recounts a time he decided to go to the dictionary to discover the definition of love. That was his first mistake. In rhyming verse, he recalls turning to the *L*'s, putting his glasses on, and—much to his apparent surprise—learning that *love* took the form of a verb. To be fair, the rapper's underlying point was that our professions of love must be backed up by action, but his second mistake was defining love solely by its outward expression.

You may agree that love is a verb. Many Christians understand love this way and cite 1 Corinthians 13:4–8 as their proof text:

> Love is patient, love is kind and is not jealous; love does not brag and is not arrogant, does not act unbecomingly; it does not seek its own, is not provoked, does not take into account a wrong suffered, does not rejoice in unrighteousness, but

---

1 DC Talk. "Luv Is A Verb." Track 1 on Free at Last. *Forefront*, 1992.

rejoices with the truth; bears all things, believes all things, hopes all things, endures all things. Love never fails.

While expressed though action, *love is not itself an action but an affectionate motivation.* Love is the underlying drive that outwardly manifests itself in behavior. Love and action are intricately linked (so much so that Paul described it as such), but there is a difference. Love will never fail to produce action, but it is not to be *strictly* equated with it. Love and patience are not exactly the same—the one causes the other. Love and kindness are not exactly the same, and so on. The deeply imbedded heart attitude of love yields these actions.

With all of that said, while we cannot have true love without action, there can most certainly be action without love. We mustn't assume biblical love is being demonstrated when actions are undertaken. Though in a limited, worldly sense, even an unbeliever can be patient, kind, longsuffering, and devoted to the service of others.

Paul's very point to the Corinthians in that passage is that one can generate "verbs" that are entirely devoid of love. In a few verses prior, he employed the outermost hypothetical extremes to prove his argument:

> If I speak with the tongues of men and of angels, but do not have love, I have become a noisy gong or a clanging cymbal. If I have the gift of prophecy, and know all mysteries and all knowledge; and if I have all faith, so as to remove mountains, but do not have love, I am nothing. And if I give all my possessions to feed the poor, and if I surrender my body to be burned, but do not have love, it profits me nothing. (1 Cor. 13:1–3)

Even the ultimate sacrifice—giving one's life—can be accomplished without true love, which strips the act of its value.

Love must precede action. Jesus told Nicodemus, "For God so loved the world, that He gave" (John 3:16). His love came before His giving. First John 3:16 echoes this: "We know love by this, that He laid down His life for us."

Flowing out of love are all kinds of verbs, but love is more than the sum of those actions. It defies a definition that is exclusively explained by the conduct it produces. Rather, love is a deep-seated state of the heart, a conviction of thought, desire, motivation, and proper affection, all rolled into one.

Love Is More Than Sacrifice and Obedience

The first half of this split branch is hard to spot because the world places the concept of self-sacrifice as the pinnacle of love. But as Paul just declared to us, sacrificial action alone does not equal love. Even when properly motivated, the love driving the sacrifice is more than the act itself.

Sacrifice that's undertaken without a passion for God; without an understanding of Him or commitment to Him; without a delight in Him or a desire to glorify Him; or without a knowledge of Christ and His work, is ultimately worthless. An unbelieving soldier can heroically jump on a grenade in the heat of battle, but if it's not directed toward God in Christ, it cannot be biblical love.

Obedience, the other half of this branch, can also be accomplished without love—just look at the Pharisees who asked Jesus about the greatest commandment. They obeyed. A lot. They made up new rules just so they could obey them! But they never loved God for a single moment. They never loved Jesus; they hated Him. Obedience, therefore, is not *necessarily* the measure of love.

Like with sacrifice, love is more than obedience but never less. Love always includes obedience. Jesus taught, "If you love Me, you will keep My commandments" (John 14:15). His disciple John learned well: "By this we know that we love the children of God, when we love God and observe His commandments. For this is the love of God, that we keep His commandments; and His commandments are not burdensome" (1 John 5:2–3). Love will always flow out in rightly motivated obedience.

Love Is Relational

The next branch is the relational aspect of love. It's personal, not clinical, cold, or mechanical. In its exercise, relationships are developed and deepened—both with God and others. We don't love *at* people; we love *toward* them. We love with the purpose of entering into relationship. Neither God nor people may be kept at arm's length. Sometimes—this may come as a surprise—people are difficult. They hurt us or irritate us, and it's hard to love them. But God does not create an allowance for, "I love you; I just don't like you," or "I'll love you—from a distance."

Rather, *love means that we are constantly pursuing and progressing into as deep a relationship as biblically appropriate with any individual in our lives at any moment.* That may be expressed very differently with each person—from limiting the ways to interact with an unrepentant church member disciplined out of the body, to the sacred intimacy of the marital bond, and everything in between. The heart's attitude is always desiring relationship.

As mentioned, Jesus revealed to Nicodemus that because God loved the world, He gave His Son in order to give eternal life to those who believe in Him (John 3:16). What is eternal life? In a prayer, Jesus explained, "This is eternal life, that they may *know* You, the only true God, and Jesus Christ whom You have sent" (John 17:3, emphasis added). God sacrificed His Son so that we could enter into a right relationship with Him. God declared, "[L] et him who boasts boast of this, that he understands and *knows Me*" (Jer. 9:24, emphasis added). This does not mean just knowing facts about God, but a personal, loving relationship with Him, made possible through the Savior.

Love Is Selfless and Humble

In 1937, Dutch painter Han van Meegeren sold a piece of art for about $4 million in today's money.[2] The high value conferred to the painting stemmed from one key point. It was presented as a painting by the seventeenth-century master Johannes Vermeer. Van Meegeren specialized in forging priceless works from the famed artist. He even fooled a leading art expert of the day. While Dr. Abraham Bredius meticulously verified the piece's supposed authenticity as a Vermeer, it was just a cheap knock-off. Even though it looked like the real thing, it wasn't. It was a fake.

Real, biblical love is selfless and humble. The world convinces itself that its version is the same caliber, but their "love" is primarily and inherently self-directed. Their love seeks reward and benefit, a return on the investment. We naturally love those who love us in return. But if this love is not motivated by our love for Christ, it's a fake. Like the art forgery, it's a cheap knock-off, even though on the surface it seems to be the real deal.

In contrast, biblical love is demonstrated toward another regardless of the receiver's response. Jesus set the bar high in His Sermon on the Mount:

> You have heard that it was said, "YOU SHALL LOVE YOUR NEIGHBOR and hate your enemy." But I say to you, love your enemies and pray for those who persecute you, so that you may be sons of your Father who is in heaven; for He causes His sun to rise on the evil and the good, and sends rain on the righteous and the unrighteous. *For if you love those who love you, what reward do you have?* Do not even the tax collectors do the same? If you greet only your brothers, what more are you doing

2 "How Mediocre Dutch Artist Cast 'The Forger's Spell'", NPR, July 12, 2008, https://www.npr.org/2008/07/12/92483237/how-mediocre-dutch-artist-cast-the-forgers-spell.
Peter Schjeldahl, "Dutch Master," *The New Yorker*, October 20, 2008, https://www.newyorker.com/magazine/2008/10/27/dutch-master.

than others? Do not even the Gentiles do the same? (Matt. 5:43–47, emphasis added)

Do you love your loved ones? There's not much credit in this instinctive response. Biblical love loves regardless of difficulty and despite being unreciprocated or even spurned. In fact, that's when love is most fully expressed. To actively love and desire good to those who set themselves against us and desire our harm fundamentally cuts against the grain of human nature—it's impossible apart from God.

Love Is Not Based on Merit

Next, love is not contingent upon merit. This branch reveals that following God's example, we do not exercise love based on the value or desirability of the object. Romans states,

> For while we were still helpless, at the right time Christ died for the ungodly. For one will hardly die for a righteous man; though perhaps for the good man someone would dare even to die. But *God demonstrates His own love toward us, in that while we were yet sinners, Christ died for us.* (Rom. 5:6–8, emphasis added)

The last verse caused the English preacher Charles Spurgeon to observe:

> [W]e were sinners against the very person who died for us. . . . [Christ] suffers for the very injury that others did to him. He dies for his enemies—dies for the men that hate and scorn him. . . .
> . . . It is quite certain that God did not consider man's merit when Christ died; in fact, no merit could have deserved the death of Jesus. Though we had been holy as Adam, we could never have deserved a sacrifice like that of Jesus for us. But

inasmuch as it says, "He died for sinners," we are thereby taught that God considered our sin, and not our righteousness. When Christ died, he died for men as black, as wicked, as abominable, not as good and excellent. Christ did not shed his blood for us as saints, but as sinners. He considered us in our loathsomeness, in our low estate and misery—not in that high estate to which grace afterwards elevates us, but in all the decay into which we had fallen by our sin. There could have been no merit in us; and therefore, God commendeth his love by our ill desert. [3]

This branch splits into two sections. When considering the reverse—our love toward God—this principle doesn't seem applicable. God does merit our love because He's perfectly good and wholly desirable, right? In reality, we love God, not on the basis of the value we believe Him to possess, but on the value He has declared Himself to possess. Do you see the difference? We don't decide God is great in our eyes and choose to love Him as a result; we love Him because He has rightfully proclaimed His own greatness. He is the perfect Object of our love and affection based on His own appraisal of Himself—not yours or mine.

Love Is Christian and Desires the Highest Good

Biblical love is always motivated by the person and work of Jesus Christ. Our love to God necessarily flows through Him; this is what makes our love uniquely "Christian." First John states, "Whoever believes that Jesus is the Christ is born of God, and whoever loves the Father loves the child born of Him" (5:1). Love is also continually

3 Charles H. Spurgeon, "Love's Commendation," sermon, New Park Street Chapel, London, November 23, 1856, transcript from New Park Street Pulpit Volume 2 Collection, The Spurgeon Center, https://www.spurgeon.org/resource-library/sermons/loves-commendation/#flipbook/.

directed toward God's glory. The highest good is for us to glorify Him, so love is directed toward this end.

Even our love for others seeks to glorify God by desiring their highest good. Love seeks the best for others at every given moment. *The highest good for every person at every moment is to be rightly related to God through Christ. Thus, to be truly loving, anything we do for another must have as its ultimate goal their conformity to Christ's image.* True love is expressed by helping others look more like Jesus. If a believer doesn't desire others to look like Christ, it's not real love. One can care for another's physical needs, but if Jesus is out of the picture, it's not biblical love. We serve, care, and share so that they will look like Jesus. We will come back to this later at length.

God showed *His* love to *us* with this same purpose: "By this the love of God was manifested in us, that God has sent His only begotten Son into the world so that we might live through Him. In this is love, not that we loved God, but that He loved us and sent His Son to be the propitiation for our sins" (1 John 4:9–10). He loved us by providing the means for us to be rightly related to Him—giving His only Son, the ultimate expression of love.

Love Finds Full Satisfaction in God

Finally, love must find full satisfaction in God alone. This branch is weighty. If our ultimate satisfaction lies in something or someone other than God, we cannot rightly claim Him as the supreme Object of our affections. *We most fully love that object from which we gain our fullest satisfaction.*

> King David exulted in God:
> You will make known to me the path of life;
> In Your presence is fullness of joy;
> In Your right hand there are pleasures forever.
> (Ps. 16:11)

Paul echoed this idea in his prayer for the Ephesians to "know the love of Christ which surpasses knowledge, that [they] may be filled up to all the fullness of God" (Eph. 3:19). He directly linked the love of Christ with full satisfaction in God. The idea that I could find more satisfaction in anything other than God and yet claim to love Him is like saying that I fully love my wife and yet find satisfaction in pornography or some other woman. It's both outrageous and preposterous. *She* is the one I love *and* in whom I am to find my satisfaction. So it must be with God.

Infinite Love for Eternity

This tree of love is taking shape. We have described only in part the main branches stemming from the trunk. The fathomless depths of love cannot be contained in this little book. Each of these major boughs has more branches bifurcating into smaller branches that, in turn, divide even further.

On top of that, consider the abundant array of blossoms, fruit, and foliage that brightly adorn the entire canopy. They may appear at first glance to be the punctuation marks to these arboreal veins of love, but upon microscopic inspection, multidimensions of fractal beauty within each individual leaf create new depths of love that can only result in joyful, overflowing worship. Thankfully, we will have eternity for such contemplations. Considering God's love for us stirs our hearts to echo the traditional hymn:

> Could we with ink the ocean fill,
> and were the skies of parchment made;
> were ev'ry stalk on earth a quill,
> and ev'ryone a scribe by trade;
> to write the love of God above
> would drain the ocean dry;
> nor could the scroll contain the whole,
> though stretched from sky to sky. [4]

Before piecing together our first definition, let's next examine the tree trunk.

---

[4] Frederick M. Lehman, "The Love of God," 1917, https://hymnary.org/text/the_love_of_god_is_greater_far.

CHAPTER 5

In Lewis Carroll's *Through the Looking Glass,* Alice encounters Humpty Dumpty. Their peculiar exchange includes a back-and-forth on the meaning of words. The cantankerous, oval-shaped nursery rhyme character replies to Alice,

> . . . "There's glory for you!"
> "I don't know what you mean by 'glory,'" Alice said. Humpty Dumpty smiled contemptuously. "Of course you don't—till I tell you. I meant 'there's a nice knock-down argument for you!'"
> "But 'glory' doesn't mean 'a nice knock-down argument,'" Alice objected.
> "When I use a word," Humpty Dumpty said in rather a scornful tone, "it means just what I choose it to mean—neither more nor less."
> "The question is," said Alice, "whether you can make words mean so many different things."[1]

---

1   Lewis Carroll (Charles Dodgson), *Through the Looking-Glass* (London: Macmillan and Co., 1871), full text accessible through the Gutenberg Project, https://www.gutenberg.org/files/12/12-h/12-h.htm.

To describe biblical love most accurately, we must understand that it has an objective meaning. We have studied the major branches of the tree and are now working our way down the trunk with a principle that has supported all the others thus far: *Love is defined by God*. We've alluded to this all throughout, but let's consider this truth for a moment before formulating a definition of love.

Love Is Defined by Scripture

Because of whom God is as the creator and embodiment of love (1 John 4:16), the source, content, direction, essence, and meaning must all come through Scripture where He discloses Himself to us. A necessary corollary to the principle that love is exclusively defined by God through Scripture is this: *Love is neither self-defined nor culturally defined.*

I don't get to choose what I think love is. I don't get to set the standard for everyone around me: "If you really love me, this is how you will relate to me." I don't get to determine when someone is or is not loving me. Neither do you. Yet culture has run amok with the idea that we define what love looks like.

The spirit of our current age insists that we affirm others' decisions and lifestyles. Anything less is unloving. Not even tolerance will suffice; celebration is demanded. Since individual expression of one's innermost desires is considered the highest virtue and the path to true happiness, refusing to affirm another's "journey" or "truth" is an act of hate. If you fail to meet others' criteria for love, you will be rejected, "canceled," and ostracized from society. You will be denied love yourself.

But neither individuals nor the culture gets to define love. God does. It behooves us, therefore, to learn precisely what love is, or even we will be swept up in the world's deceptive ideas and become convinced that what is unloving is loving and vice versa.

In 2019, Starbucks released a commercial to express their support of the transgender lifestyle.[2] Designed to tug at the heartstrings, the ad opens with a young girl presenting as male. Much to her chagrin, in various social settings her given name Jemma is used: for an application, at the doctor's office, on her student ID card, with her parents, and so on. The bleak, monochromatic scenes with somber piano accompaniment stir the heart toward compassion for this girl who is clearly struggling and hurting.

The resolution comes when Jemma enters a Starbucks, orders a coffee, and the barista asks for her name on the order. After she thoughtfully replies, "James," the worker appears to happily comply. Just as we have all experienced ourselves, the name is written across the cup's side, leaving us to wonder what harm could possibly be done in indulging Jemma's deluded desires. The viewer even witnesses a little smile of hope break across the girl's face as her assumed identity is validated. Commenting on its ad, the coffee company declared: "[W]riting your name on a cup and calling it out is a symbol of our warm welcome. It's . . . symbolic of what we believe in: [r]ecognition and acceptance, whoever you are, or want to be. We welcome everyone."

This is an example of the world's idea of love. Conversely, the culture is also declaring a lack of approval as hatred. Simply refraining from comment is considered "violence."[3] While broadening their definition of love, their tolerance for anything outside of those boundaries narrows accordingly. We are witnessing the utter debauchery that results when love is unhitched from its biblical moorings. Anything—and culture is truly moving toward anything—can be called love.

---

2 Starbucks UK, "Starbucks LGBT+ Channel 4 Diversity Award 2019 | Every name's a story (Extended Version)," YouTube video, February 2, 2020, Starbucks UK, https://www.youtube.com/watch?v=pcSP1r9eCWw.
3 Jeannine Gramick, "We need a victory of speech over the violence of silence," *National Catholic Reporter*, July 11, 2016, https://www.ncronline.org/we-need-victory-speech-over-violence-silence.

But God is the One who gets to set the boundaries. Who gave the culture, the courts, or a couple the authority to define love? God did not cede this divine right. The God who "made the world and all things in it" decides the meaning of love (Acts 17:24)—not finite creatures with feeble understandings, broken emotions, and sinful proclivities. Love is not subjective or relative, varying from person to person, culture to culture, or moment to moment. Love is objective, and the universal standard is found in Scripture alone.

A Defining Moment

At long last, we've come to the tree's roots. Let's construct from these biblical principles our first definition. Remember we will have two definitions based on the dual commands to love God and love our neighbor. These two loves are interconnected, but it's helpful to define them separately. That said, let's start with defining our primary love toward God:

> ***Love to God*** **is the Holy Spirit-empowered affection and motivation to delight in an intimate relationship with Him through Christ by humbly doing everything commanded in Scripture to glorify Him and find our full satisfaction in Him without thought of the cost to us or what we might receive in return.**

To achieve a comprehensive definition, we clearly have a lot going on here. Let's break it down:

- *Holy Spirit-empowered affection and motivation—* This is a heart affection which longs for Him. It can be reflected emotionally in different ways at different times, or sometimes not at all. The Spirit drives it, so this makes it supernatural and exclusive to believers.

44

- *Delight in intimate relationship with Him*— This is a desire to be deeply bonded and closely connected to God.

- *Through Christ*—The desire for relationship is impossible because of our sin, but through the person and work of Christ, He provides the way for the impossible to become possible.

- *In humility*—As we've already seen, you cannot love someone else out of arrogance. We must cultivate a proper view of ourselves in light of who God is in His greatness in order to properly love Him.

- *In accordance with the principles of Scripture*— Since God defines love, we love according to what He says in His Word. There's no true love outside of *His* definition.

- *To bring Him glory*—Love always desires to bring to God what is appropriately due Him. This must be our chief aim.

- *Finding full satisfaction in Him alone*—This is the primary way we accomplish glorifying God. He graciously wraps up our own highest good in the pursuit of His.

- *Total sacrifice and selflessness*—This is not the *quid pro quo* love of the world. Because our delight is in pursuing God, we obey His commands, yield to His desires, and worship Him alone. While Christ did call us to measure the cost as it pertains to salvation (Luke 14:25-33), we love God for who He is.

This is the Christian life. This is what it means to love God. This is the context for His commands and our obedience. It should be clear that—as we said from the outset—it's supernatural. How could *anyone* even approach *anything* that slightly resembles this kind of love without the very power of the Spirit of God inside him?

When God saves sinners, He places in them the Holy Spirit who loves the Father and the Son (1 John 4:13). In turn, the Spirit testifies with the Christian's own spirit and strengthens him through the Word to love in the same way. But it's only possible through Him: No human being, no natural man, no unbeliever could ever love in this way. That's why the Bible declares that *love is a defining mark of a Christian.*

We fail to demonstrate this love perfectly and consistently, but that's the command. We love Him with everything that we are. It's what we live for—our reason for being. Our love for God identifies us above all other things as belonging to Him. It is first and foremost. Even our love for others flows out from this foundational love to Him, as we will soon see. Loving our neighbors is representative of our love for God.

This Spirit-empowered delight is a consuming passion for God, a continual pursuit of Him, and a whole-hearted, scripturally-grounded devotion. Paul stated that Christians love Jesus with "incorruptible love" (Eph. 6:24). Love of that caliber does not originate from us but is from God, empowered by the Spirit to be given back to Him for His glory. On the flip side, 1 Corinthians states, "If anyone does not love the Lord, he is to be accursed" (16:22). This love creates a clear distinction between the empowered believer and the powerless unbeliever.

For believers, this means that love like this *is* possible! It is to be pursued and exercised. Far from an abstract idea, this manner of love resounds into eternity. He is worth all our consuming love. We may have other loves, but they are all sub-loves.

As you consider these truths, your soul may be rejoicing in hearty assent, but practically speaking, does your life as well? Self-examination here is critical. Let me conclude this chapter with a few questions to help you prayerfully evaluate your heart:

- Would you say that your life is defined by your love for God, or are there other affections that compete for top placement? Perhaps a greater love for family, self, work, pleasure, or something else? We can easily mask these attachments— *especially* the good ones—and deceive ourselves. The Pharisees were guilty of this. They knew the Old Testament. They memorized and quoted Scripture. They knew the commands. They believed they loved God and that their strict adherence to the law and traditions signified as much. But their avowed love was proved false by their outright rejection of the Son of God as their Messiah. They refused to bend the knee to the One who would topple their cherished systems. For them, their idolatrous love was the praise of men. Do you have similar idols that are supplanting God's position as the supreme Object worthy of your affections?

- Do you delight in knowing God? Sure, this takes effort, but the exertion is driven by the blessing of enjoying relationship with your gracious, loving Creator. Judging by the time you invest in this relationship, how would an outside observer assess your delight? The best way to cultivate this craving for the "pure milk of the word" is to start imbibing it now (1 Pet. 2:2).

- Relatedly, are you finding your satisfaction in God? Perhaps your love is cold because you've been seeking satisfaction elsewhere. As a result, your love for God may be slowly diminishing like a leaky bucket that can't retain water (Jer. 2:13).

- Are you pursuing the knowledge of God? Maybe you're missing the continual refreshment and reminders of God's character that His Word unfailingly supplies. While your heart may soar on Sunday mornings, you might be neglecting your pursuit of Him throughout the week. If you're not actively and continually considering Him, it may be why your love is cold and weak.

- Are you laying down your life for Him? You may be lacking in love because you're refusing to sacrifice. Is there anything you're holding onto with which you refuse to part? Bitterness? Anger? Lack of love for another? What you run to for comfort? Forgiveness? Pornography? Media? Unless you loosen that grip and yield to God's authority, your love will cool.

- Are you focusing on loving God through Christ? You may not be fully appreciating Christ and His provision that makes love to the Father possible. Are you regularly preaching the gospel to yourself?

We probably all feel convicted by one or more of these questions. We will never fully love God to this degree of comprehensiveness at every moment. Our indwelling sin that remains attempts to thwart us at every turn. But God has given us every resource to succeed. Our hearts yearn to love Him fully. Even as we fail to live it out perfectly, we desire to ever increasingly grow in our love for Him.

Maybe you profess to know God, dear reader, and upon close inspection, you find no real love for Him in your heart. Repent and believe for the first time, taking hold of Christ's provision so that you *can* experience this kind of love. Pursue Him. You can't lose! Place this love on top of everything else. It's the first and foremost commandment. Press into your obedience of this command and see what God will do in your life and the lives of those around you.

CHAPTER 6

When it comes to love, culture has its own spectrum of perspectives. On one end, many desperately cling to their own ideas of love, but they're only illusions. They grasp for a satisfaction and depth always out of reach. As a result, dramatic declarations ultimately ring hollow and flat:

- "True love doesn't have to come to you. It has to be inside you."

- "Love is space and time measured by the heart."

- "You are the one you've been waiting for."

- "We loved with a love that was more than love."

- "Love is composed of a single soul inhabiting two bodies."

- "To love oneself is the beginning of a lifelong romance."[1]

---

1 BrainyQuote, s.v. "love," accessed January 26, 2023, https://www.brainyquote.com/search_results?q=love. Multiple quotations were pulled from this source.

- "Love is a lesson taught to us by others; the truth of life; the light that guides us through our darkest hours; a calm and peaceful feeling; neither reward, not punishment; has no bounds or restrictions.[2]

On the other end, some may sense the shallow reality of such professions and opt for a sardonic cynicism that mocks the world's deficient and disappointing attempts:

- "Love is an ocean of emotions entirely surrounded by expenses."[3]

- "I love being married. It's so great to find one special person you want to annoy for the rest of your life."

- "Love is the only kind of fire which is never covered by insurance."

- "Love is the triumph of imagination over intelligence."

- "When one is in love, one always begins by deceiving one's self, and one always ends by deceiving others. That is what the world calls a romance."

- "Love conquers all things except poverty and toothache."[4]

2 Urban Dictionary, s.v. "love," accessed January 26, 2023, https://www.urbandictionary.com/define.php?term=Love. Definition is a distilled version of the original; edited for length.
3 "Funny Love Quotes," Luvze, May 29, 2018, https://www.luvze.com/funny-love-quotes/.
4 "Cynical Love Quotes," AZ Quotes, accessed January 26, 2023, https://www.azquotes.com/quotes/topics/cynical-love.html. Multiple quotations were pulled form this source.

It's hardly surprising that the world is confused about love. Satan has tirelessly worked to cloud minds and spread lies. Just listen to pop music, watch television, or view a Disney movie. He's done everything possible to obscure love by hijacking the term to mean anything but biblical love.

Sadly, as we've already seen, his machinations extend into the church. Because love is the primary command for the Christian, he seeks to taint it, thereby impeding our growth and utility to God. Our society is understandably befuddled, but if Christians misunderstand love, we misunderstand what it means to be Christian. We cannot allow the world's preoccupation with unbiblical love to influence us.

We must remember that we are united to Christ because He loved us. From before the beginning of time, He set His love upon us and drew us to Himself to both know *and* love Him (Eph. 1:4–5). We learned in the last chapter that He called us to Himself so we can properly love Him, the Lord our God. But as we'll see in this chapter, He's also called us to *love others* because that's what He does. His very nature is to love, and so it must be for those He has transformed. *The world must know we are Christians by our love* (John 13:35). What a tremendous disservice to our God if we are not marked by this. We were not created to simply obey God and live with others; we were made to love God *and* love others.

Second Best

American pole vaulter Earle Meadows earned gold for his country in the 1936 Summer Olympics held in Berlin. Second place was not as clear. Two athletes tied, clearing the exact same height. Both from Japan, Shuhei Nishida and Sueo Oe requested that the judges award them each a silver medal. They refused, leaving the two men to work out who would receive the silver and who would take the bronze.

53

Their precise agreement was undoubtedly revealed upon their return home. Visiting a jeweler, they had each medal cut in half and welded to the other piece. This resulted in two similar medals, later dubbed the "Medals of Friendship."[5] While neither man was the greatest, the next greatest position was of great import to them. Even though someone once observed, "No one remembers who came in second,"[6] Jesus did. When asked to name the greatest commandment, Jesus found "second place" to be so critical (and related, as we will see), He included it in His response.

Answering the lawyer's question, Jesus punctuated His reply by concluding, "This is the great and foremost commandment" (Matt. 22:38). Done. Answered. But the second greatest was so vital and so inextricably linked to the first, Christ mentioned it. He continued: "The second is like it, 'YOU SHALL LOVE YOUR NEIGHBOR AS YOURSELF.' On these two commandments depend the whole Law and the Prophets" (22:39–40).

In fact, they are so integrally connected, you can't pull them apart. Even though the first takes precedence, you can't have one without the other. The primary component of a biblical love for God is a love that's expressed toward His created humanity. Scripture is clear: *You cannot have a love for God and not love the people whom He made in His image* (1 John 4:20).

Let's first consider what Jesus meant by observing that "[t]he second is like it." How is loving our neighbors similar to loving God? To say it was "like" the first, Jesus used a Greek term that meant a resemblance in appearance, character, or nature. It was in the same manner. Even though it's not foremost, the second

5 Cezary Jan Strusiewicz, "Medals of Friendship: The Heartwarming Story of the 1936 Olympics," *Tokyo Weekender*, July 20, 2021, https://www.tokyoweekender.com/2021/07/medals-friendship-heartwarming-story-1936-summer-olympics/.

6 Isaias Lijauco, "8 Things You Didn't Know About Walter Hagen," *Let's Golf Better*, February 12, 2022, https://letsgolfbetter.com/8-things-you-didnt-know-about-walter-hagen/?expand_article=1. Lijauco is quoting Walter Hagen.

precept is of similar magnitude because it is the primary expression of the first. They must go together.

The relationship between faith and works may be a useful analogy. John Calvin argued, "It is therefore faith alone which justifies, and yet the faith which justifies is not alone."[7] Like James, he was pointing out that while faith is the prime mover and works in no way contribute to our salvation, they still serve as necessary evidence of faith's effective existence.

Likewise, biblically loving others is an outflow of our love for God. We cannot truly love our neighbors if we don't truly love God; and if we truly love God, this will always produce love for our neighbors. *To love one another is to love God.* Remember that "[w]e love, because He first loved us" (1 John 4:19). Loving God motivates us to accomplish His will for the benefit of others. Exercising our love for Him is the highest good we can give those around us. Loving God drives our godliness. As we increasingly reflect His character, we will better relate to people. We will care for them more and more like God cares for them.

The connection between the two is so interlinked, John declared: "If someone says, 'I love God,' and hates his brother, he is a liar; for the one who does not love his brother whom he has seen, cannot love God whom he has not seen. And this commandment we have from Him, that the one who loves God should love his brother also" (1 John 4:20–21). John doesn't pull any punches. If you love God, you will love others.

Our love for others does not create a love for God; rather, it demonstrates the reality of it, which originates with God Himself—"In this is love, not that we loved God, but that He loved us and sent His Son to be the propitiation for our sins" (1 John 4:10). Because believers love God, everything they think and do—consider and decide—should be tied to their love for others.

---

7   John Calvin, *Acts of the Council of Trent with the Antidote* (1547), full text accessible through Monergism.com, https://www.monergism.com/threshold/sdg/calvin_trentantidote.html.

In fact, we will see how it is that "[o]n these two commands depend the whole Law and the Prophets" (v. 40). They both lay the framework for every other commandment contained in His Word because Scripture is the sum total of love—but more on that later. For now, before we decipher what the second commandment means, we need to first address what it does *not* mean.

Love Thyself?

In the greatest commandment, Jesus described love for God as all-encompassing—with the totality of our being. He called for that kind of love toward others as well but didn't use the same depiction of heart, soul, and mind. Instead, He used a comparison. Quoting from Leviticus 19:18, Jesus reminded the Pharisees they were to love their neighbors according to the manner in which they loved themselves. Self-love is a comprehensive love, too, but we cannot assume because it's man's instinctive bent that Jesus—or God's law for that matter—is in *any* way commending or commanding it.

Sadly, many have misunderstood this verse. They have interpreted it to mean that loving yourself is just as important as love to God and neighbor—even more so, since they infer self-love must exist before loving others is even possible. *This is a satanic inversion of Jesus' teaching, and all Christians must reject it wholesale.*

In reality, Christ was merely observing man's natural proclivity to protect himself, provide for himself, take care of himself, and all around do what he thinks is best for himself. We were built this way. While exercising care over our person is a responsibility God gave mankind as stewards, man's wicked nature immediately twists it into sinful selfishness and self-centered indulgence. This self-love is always there. Even to the furthest extents of self-loathing like suicide, selfish desires still drive those decisions.

For the believer whose old nature has been destroyed and the power of sin broken, love of self is still always evident. As long as we're breathing, we love ourselves. It's instinctive. It's continual.

A seminary professor once recounted counseling a college student who claimed she suffered from not loving herself enough. In fact, according to her, she hated herself. One day he spotted her at the school cafeteria. He observed her at the salad bar, rifling through a large bowl of cherry tomatoes. What was she doing? "She hates herself," the professor playfully suggested, "so she's looking for the worst cherry tomatoes in the bunch to put on her salad."[8] Of course, the opposite was true. Because of her default nature, she was picking out the best ones for herself. That's what we all do.

It's wholehearted. You love yourself *with* all yourself. Your whole inner man loves you. This is all Jesus is saying here. It's what we do. The implications of the comparison, then, are huge—this is how the renewed, transformed heart of the believer should be toward others: instinctive, continual, wholehearted devotion. Our very spiritual DNA should be to love others in this way.

Paul commanded, "Do nothing from selfishness or empty conceit, but with humility of mind regard one another as more important than yourselves" (Phil. 2:3). That doesn't sound like the modern self-esteem movement, does it? In fact, it's quite the reverse. Paul continued, "[D]o not merely look out for your own personal interests, but also for the interests of others" (v. 4). Echoing Jesus, Paul implied that we naturally *do* look out for our own interests. The desire to have our needs met is inescapable.

Many have distorted Jesus' words. We cannot quickly move past this point as the world has infected the church with this insidious lie. The world pays the piper, calling for the tune "Love Yourself" to be played, and the mainstream church eagerly agrees to dance. They manipulate and contort Scripture to reflect the world by affirming the necessity of being all about the self before we can be about everyone else. They click on the phrase "as yourself" and

---

8   Dr. John Street, "Counseling Blended Families 2," lecture, MP3 audio, The Institute of Biblical Counseling and Discipleship, https://ibcd.org/Series/counseling-blended-families-ss08/.

drag it to the very top of the list of commandments. They claim we must first learn to love ourselves, as though we needed instructions.

They equate this directly with self-esteem—a consuming self-preoccupation that can be expressed across a spectrum. Self-absorption can range from the unsurprising egotistical braggart all the way to the insecure, self-harming, angsty loner. Both inordinately focus on themselves. Both are built on pride: either the self-congratulatory elation of "I deserve this!" or the fist-brandishing, implied "I deserve better!" and everything in between.

Their "esteem"—their estimation of their own value—may be high or low, but their eyes are both fixed inwardly on themselves. Their hearts sit on their own thrones to make their own evaluations. "[L]overs of self" is a description included in a laundry list of wicked sins perpetrated by false teachers (2 Tim. 3:2); the Bible never commends it. By no means is low self-esteem "self-lessness," true biblical humility that focuses on and fears God rather than men. The Bible teaches that everyone's natural consideration of himself is full (Rom. 3:18; 12:3; Isa. 5:21; Gal. 6:3). We are all truly full of ourselves.

In contrast to what Scripture says, these purveyors of self-love claim that people don't have *enough* self-esteem. They must learn to develop it, they argue, before they can love God or others. Based on a worldly understanding of love, these leaders in the church claim that people are truly lacking in a care for themselves. This self-love can be rightly defined as *viewing oneself as having the highest value in relationship to others by working to ensure one's own greatest good*. Needs for survival, security, pleasure, and purpose are all viewed as one's greatest good.

Sadly, much of Christian counseling has bought into psychology's lie lock, stock, and barrel. This is why mixing man's supposed wisdom with God's wisdom is so deadly. Reams of books line Christian bookstores, touting the crucial need to fill up your love cup with self-care. Consequently (and tragically), believers join the world in pursuing these self-oriented desires, trusting that a true love for others is just around the corner. But the more they seek to cultivate their self-love apart from a proper understanding of biblical love, the more that a love for God and others will forever elude them.

In the summer of 1827, British explorer Edward Parry led an expedition to the North Pole.[9] He and his crew met with crushing setbacks that ultimately forced them to turn back. Slowing down to a crawl, they slogged through slushy ice water while towing heavy, equipment-laden sledges on a fraction of the caloric intake required as the sun's refracted rays induced snow blindness. Shockingly, that wasn't the worst of it. While charting their position against the stars, Parry learned that their dragging progress had somehow *lost* ground—the ice field underneath them was flowing southward at a faster rate than they were traveling north. Despite their strenuous efforts, they were heading in the opposite direction! That is exactly how far loving yourself will lead you toward a love for God and others.

Perception Correction

Our improper view of ourselves can only be corrected by a proper view of God. It must start here. We must first understand the greatness of His character and nature in order to have proper *humility*—the antidote to constant self-engrossment. We must humble ourselves "under the mighty hand of God" (1 Pet. 5:6), looking outside ourselves to understand who we truly are—broken, apart from Him.

True fulfillment includes an accurate assessment of ourselves in light of who He is. The Holy Spirit opens our eyes to this reality through the power of the Word. Believers are enabled to give of themselves to God and to others. *It is as we give that we are truly filled—not that we must first be filled so that we can truly give.*

---

9 Kat Long, "Go North, Young Man," January 22, 2021 (updated July 27, 2022), episode 2 in The Quest for the North Pole, produced by Mental Floss, podcast, transcript, https://www.mentalfloss.com/article/639725/quest-for-the-north-pole-episode-2-podcast-transcript.

Paul recalled his former condition of life before Christ, and it was rife with self-esteem:

> If anyone else has a mind to put confidence in the flesh, I far more: circumcised the eighth day, of the nation of Israel, of the tribe of Benjamin, a Hebrew of Hebrews; as to the Law, a Pharisee; as to zeal, a persecutor of the church; as to the righteousness which is in the Law, found blameless. (Phil. 3:4–6)

His highest point of self-esteem was his furthest point away from God.

Relinquishing his precious ego and exchanging it for "Christ-esteem," Paul recognized that those accomplishments had only earned him further condemnation. Instead, he reveled in the value of being "found in Him, not having a righteousness of [his] own derived from the Law, but that which is through faith in Christ" (3:9). As a redeemed sinner, Paul gloried in Christ, not himself! We too must learn to grow our "Christ-esteem."

A Warning for Warmth

We must, however, guard against any pendulum swings that pull us from the precision offered by a sound, biblical anthropology. While Scripture clearly reveals fallen man in his unregenerate condition to be inherently wicked and spiritually dead, we do not take this vertical position before God and apply it horizontally to our fellow man in relationships. The Bible is clear that we ought to highly esteem both God *and* our fellow man. Only on ourselves must we think little.

Just because men are vile, foolish, contemptible, rebellious worms before God, spiritually speaking, this in no way means *we* can treat them accordingly on a relational plane. Despite man's condemnation by God, we are *all* created in His image. We must make this careful distinction. There is double value conferred to us—even unbelievers—because we are God's creatures *and* made in His likeness. We must be so careful that in trying to get away from this unbiblical idea of self-esteem, we don't misunderstand and forsake our esteem for others. While only believers are God's spiritual children, we are all God's image-bearers. James puts this to bed with his warnings about harmful speech:

> But no one can tame the tongue; it is a restless evil and full of deadly poison. With it we bless our Lord and Father, and with it we curse men, *who have been made in the likeness of God*; from the same mouth come both blessing and cursing. My brethren, these things ought not to be this way. (James 3:8–10, emphasis added)

These "men" made in God's likeness include everyone—even those who do horrible things. We recognize the evil that comes forth from their inherent corruption and deal with it appropriately, all while maintaining the honor due to them as God's image-bearers.

Addressing the Athenians on Mars Hill, Paul acknowledged that through God, believers and unbelievers alike "live and move and exist, as even some of [their] own poets have said, 'For we also are His children'" (Acts 17:28). Before establishing the need for repentance to be God's spiritual children, Paul made clear we are all His creation.

Holding onto the truths of this chapter, then, let's now move forward in understanding our next object of love—our neighbor.

CHAPTER 7

Before defining *love to God* in chapter 3, we examined the Object of our affections—the Lord our God whom we are commanded to love. Likewise, we should define the object of our love before considering *love to neighbor*. Other than Mister Rogers, who is our neighbor? Thankfully, someone already asked Jesus this exact question.

Won't You Be My Neighbor?

As we've been walking through this attempted setup by the Pharisees, we mentioned earlier that their final question was a bit anticlimactic, since it was quite similar to another that had already been posed by yet another lawyer. Luke 10 captures this conversation:

> And a lawyer stood up and put Him to the test, saying, "Teacher, what shall I do to inherit eternal life?" And He said to him, "What is written in the Law? How does it read to you?" And he answered, "You shall love the Lord your God with

ALL YOUR HEART, AND WITH ALL YOUR SOUL,
AND WITH ALL YOUR STRENGTH, AND WITH
ALL YOUR MIND; AND YOUR NEIGHBOR AS
YOURSELF." And He said to him, "You have
answered correctly; DO THIS AND YOU WILL LIVE"
But wishing to justify himself, he said to Jesus, "And
who is my neighbor?" (Luke 10:25–29)

Interestingly, this lawyer was asking for directions to heaven,
much like the rich, young ruler. The answer? Keeping the greatest
commandment and its close second. Ironically, Jesus had the lawyer
answer his own question based on his interpretation of the law. We
should not be unimpressed here. He put these two commands from
Deuteronomy 6 and Leviticus 19 together, ostensibly on his own.

Jesus affirmed the response and even encouraged him to
go and try his hand at loving God wholly and perfectly while
simultaneously loving others in the same way he continually cared
for himself every single moment. You have to wonder what's going
on in the lawyer's head at this point. Perhaps he felt by answering
this theological question astutely, he was already halfway there.
Knowing was half the battle, and he figured it out. Living it should
be a piece of cake. But he must have already been thinking of
some people he deemed undeserving of his total care. He needed
an out for those. That's why Luke says he was seeking to "justify
himself" (v. 29).

Even though the passage began with the lawyer trying to test
Jesus, he immediately sensed that the tables had turned. *His* life
was now under examination. Perhaps he was truly asking Jesus
where the boundaries of his "neighborhood" extended. If Jesus
would just limit this love to those of His chosen people who act
in a similar, neighborly fashion, he would have been set!

Much to his chagrin, it would seem, Jesus answered with
a parable:

Jesus replied and said, "A man was going down from Jerusalem to Jericho, and fell among robbers, and they stripped him and beat him, and went away leaving him half dead. And by chance a priest was going down on that road, and when he saw him, he passed by on the other side. Likewise a Levite also, when he came to the place and saw him, passed by on the other side. But a Samaritan, who was on a journey, came upon him; and when he saw him, he felt compassion, and came to him and bandaged up his wounds, pouring oil and wine on them; and he put him on his own beast, and brought him to an inn and took care of him. On the next day he took out two denarii and gave them to the innkeeper and said, 'Take care of him; and whatever more you spend, when I return I will repay you.' Which of these three do you think proved to be a neighbor to the man who fell into the robbers' hands?" And he said, "The one who showed mercy toward him." Then Jesus said to him, "Go and do the same." (Luke 10:30–37)

As He had done on previous occasions, Jesus used an outrageous illustration to highlight His point. Knowing how much Jews despised "half-bred" Samaritans, you would think that Jesus would cast the Samaritan to be the injured party in the story. That would be jaw-dropping enough, but it seems from the text the victim is simply a fellow Jew. Even more shocking, He chose the Samaritan to be the rescuer *over and against* Jews who were the most likely candidates to exhibit godly love. Neither the priest nor the Levite exercised love to God or neighbor in His story.

Samaritans—Jews who had intermarried with past conquering nations—were repulsive and disgusting to the Jews. They reviled them with the utmost racial hatred. They refused to have any dealings with them whatsoever, and the feeling was quite mutual. The exuberant, over-the-top demonstration of love by the Samaritan, then, starkly contrasted with the cold, selfish behavior of the priest and the Levite. It compelled the lawyer to reluctantly admit who had shown the victim true care.

When Christ implored the lawyer to meet that standard, he should have honestly concluded that he is incapable of producing that kind of love. Unregenerate man cannot keep God's law perfectly or in any possible way that could please Him. In no way was Christ merely issuing a moral command for people to do better in hopes of attaining heaven.

Notice in Jesus' story that the emphasis was not on the Jewish victim as the neighbor in need but on the Samaritan acting the part of neighbor through his actions. It's a two-way street. We *have* neighbors, and we ourselves *are* neighbors. We *become* neighbors to anyone and everyone upon whom we bestow mercy—regardless of race, appearance, gender, wealth, lovability, proximity, mutual affection, etc. Thus, the question of who our neighbor *is* becomes: Who needs mercy? *Everybody.* Who needs compassion? *Everybody. Everyone is our neighbor.*

Everyone includes difficult people. Everyone includes people who don't love us back. Everyone includes deranged sociopaths who mercilessly gun down children in schools; or angry women who obnoxiously flaunt their right to have babies in their wombs torn asunder; or cross-dressing men in hyper-sexualized outfits who voice their heinous propaganda to your community's youth; or hate-filled terrorists who celebrate the deaths of Americans.

While we need wisdom and biblical principles to determine how love for each person is to be expressed, they are all our neighbors, even if they don't respond to our love. Scripture helps us to know how to interact and relate to our neighbors lovingly. We must have a properly motivated love for everyone, from those remotest to us to those closest to us.

The sad reality is we don't. We begin to segment our social circles in the church and in other areas of life. We begin to make excuses and slowly surround ourselves with only those who treat us well; or are our age and stage in life; or have the same parenting approaches, political views, or pet hobbies. We must demonstrate love to those who are furthest away on the outer edges before we can be assured that we will truly love the people in our proximity well. As Jesus already said, "[I]f you love those who love you, what reward do you have?" (Matt. 5:46).

Another Defining Moment

At last, we've come to our next definition based on what the Bible teaches. We've already defined *love to God* in chapter 5, so let's now construct a definition for *love to neighbor*:

> **Love to neighbor is the Holy Spirit-empowered affection and motivation to delight in relationship with others, which causes us to humbly obey every command of Scripture, so that they would be continually conformed to the image of Christ, regardless of the sacrifice necessary and without any thought of what we might receive in return.**

Can you see the similarities to the greatest commandment? If you love the Lord your God, you can, must, and do love others. They are linked. We cannot be like the lawyer in Luke who tried to justify why he didn't love certain people. To love is to desire the other's highest good, and *the highest good for anyone—believer or unbeliever—is to know, love, and be conformed to the image of Christ.* This extends from the people who sit in the world's seats of power to those who sit next to you in the seats around your dinner table.

Content is King

In 2003, an email with an optical illusion of sorts went viral. It read, in part:

> Aoccdrnig to a rscheerear at Cmabrigde Uinervtisy, it deosn't mttaer in waht oredr the ltteers in a wrod are, the olny iprmoetnt tihng is taht the frist and lsat ltteer be at the rghit pclae. The rset can be a toatl mses and you can sitll raed it wouthit porbelm. Tihs is bcuseae the huamn mnid deos not raed ervey lteter by istlef, but the wrod as a wlohe.[1]

Were you surprised that you could read this? We might hastily conclude that the jumbled letters in the middle are utterly irrelevant—that we only need the two that bookend each word, but that's not *entirely* true, is it? Even though the letters in the middle can be shuffled around, we still need the right letters. If we insert any letter we want inside each word, the trick won't work. Nothing can be understood. *The content still matters.*

Similarly, the content of our love is crucial. It's critical that we fill it in correctly. Looking up *love* in Merriam-Webster's, I found several definitions. Look at their content: "A strong affection for another arising out of kinship or personal ties; attraction based on sexual desire; affection based on admiration, benevolence, or common interests; warm attachment, enthusiasm, or devotion; unselfish, loyal, and benevolent concern for the good of another."[2]

There are some good components to these definitions, but it's difficult to precisely understand what "affection" and "warm attachment" mean. But the content of these definitions has nothing remotely to do with whom? *Christ.* As we've already stated—and

---

1 "If Yuo're Albe To Raed Tihs, You Might Have Typoglycemia," Dictionary.com, August 15, 2022, https://www.dictionary.com/e/typoglycemia/. There was a mistake in the original (explained in the link) that was corrected in my citation.
2 Merriam-Webster.com Dictionary, s.v. "love," accessed January 26, 2023, https://www.merriam-webster.com/dictionary/love.

it bears repeating—we must begin with who God is and what He's done. Yet so often I hear preachers and congregants give worldly definitions of love dressed up in spiritual language.

To simply state that love is someone's highest good, or that it's unconditional, for example, is to let others fill in the content with their own ideas of those things. We are guilty of this, too. If love to God and neighbor are the two greatest commandments, *we need to be so clear on exactly what love is.* What do you mean precisely when you say, "I love you"? Do you even know? How can we demonstrate love well if our understanding is vague and tinged with worldly error? How will we be able to give our all in pursuing it? How will we be able to teach our children what love is? *Content matters.*

Consider, for instance, Christ's command to love our enemies (Matt. 5:43–48). It is imperative that we know what properly loving people who hate God looks like; otherwise, we may wind up aiding and abetting their sin and dishonoring God in the process. Do you see how critical this is? If our understanding of love is infected with worldly notions, we will end up in serious trouble.

Every time we talk about love, we need to be understanding it biblically. Both the framework *and* the content should be thoroughly and wholly biblical. We must know love inside and out because the world fills in its own content. They are convinced your exclusive insistence on Christ is patently unloving. They will accuse you of disrupting the very peace you supposedly bring. While the minds of the unbelieving are blinded by the god of this world (2 Cor. 4:4), we must be crystal clear on the meaning of love.

Loving the local man who dresses up in flamboyant gowns at your library to read lies to kids *includes* rejection of his behavior and appropriate indignation at the library for allowing it. It also includes compassionately addressing his sin and directing him to Christ, should the opportunity be provided. Strong words may be required, as Jesus had for the Pharisees; but the point is, unless we have the proper biblical content to our love, we will end up harming, rather than helping, the cause of Christ. It may be twisted into either improper tolerance on the one hand or improper condemnation on the other. Sadly, this has been repeatedly demonstrated in the American church. "Love" devolves into either vitriolic, divisive tweets on the one side or rainbow flags festooning church buildings on the other. In reality, both terminate in lovelessness.

In the next chapter, let's break down our newest definition, so that we can ensure we're getting the right content.

CHAPTER 8

During the holiday shopping season of 2018, a select group of stylish social media influencers arrived at *Palessi*—a chic, new boutique in Santa Monica, California—for an invitation-only event replete with champagne, cameras, and bass-pumping beats.[1] Featuring high-end fashionable footwear, the store captured the trendsetters' excited reactions to their sleek heels, sneakers, and boots. Many interviewed estimated the value of the shoes to be somewhere between $300 and $600 a pop. *Palessi* raked in several thousand dollars from the two-day promotional opening.

A few days later, the event was revealed to be a clever marketing ploy by none other than Payless Shoes, the bourgeois discount shoe chain typically located in outlet malls with messy shelving and fraying carpets. Their friendly social experiment of sorts boasted an *1,800 percent* markup as the glitterati were fawning over $19.99

---

1 Jordan Valinsky, "Payless fools influencers with a fake store," CNN, November 29, 2018, https://www.cnn.com/2018/11/29/business/payless-fake-store/index.html.
Jeff Swystun, "Palessi is an Indictment of Our Times," *Medium*, December 12, 2018, https://jeffswystun.medium.com/palessi-is-an-indictment-of-our-times-a234bfdba671.

pumps and running shoes. The fooled fashionistas were misled by a veneer of top-notch value. The lack of quality in the shoe itself was more than offset by its flashy presentation.

Similarly, we can be taken in by what looks like love on the surface. Though it can come attractively packaged as the real deal, we can still be duped. What we need is the utmost discernment to spot superficial knockoffs, while also ensuring that our *own* love is not found to be void of true depth.

Summing It Up, Breaking It Down

We have two definitions now. In chapter 5, we defined love to the Lord our God:

> **Love to God** is the Holy Spirit-empowered affection and motivation to delight in an intimate relationship with Him through Christ by humbly doing everything commanded in Scripture to glorify Him and find our full satisfaction in Him without thought of the cost to us or what we might receive in return.

In the last chapter, we learned that we are also called to love anyone who needs mercy—i.e. every other person on earth. We defined it as:

> **Love to neighbor** is the Holy Spirit-empowered affection and motivation to delight in relationship with others, which causes us to humbly obey every command of Scripture, so that they would be continually conformed to the image of Christ, regardless of the sacrifice necessary and without any thought of what we might receive in return.

You'll notice that these definitions are similar since they are interconnected. The love is the same; it's just directed in a different way to a different object. Both loves are generated by God. Both are rooted in God's law given in the Old Testament.

I've worked on these definitions of love over the years because my love is weak, and I've seen that love is also weak in others. What a tragedy if people walk into a church and say, "This looks just like my CrossFit community." No one will be transformed by a church like that. Rather, we want them to be radically changed by the supernatural content of our love.

Anyone can be friendly. Anyone can be nice. But *real* love is powerful. If the one thing we're supposed to do is love God and love others, we'd better know what it means. We can fall so short, so we must constantly work through this and keep it front and center because we must love well. It's the *one* thing we're commanded to do. If we truly desire for our churches to reflect God properly—and we should—the only way to pursue that end is through love to God and neighbor.

Love is Supernatural

Like our love to God, our love to neighbor *must* be supernatural; otherwise, it's impossible. Only believers can truly love God and their fellow man wholeheartedly because of the change that God has wrought in their hearts. Jesus alluded to the total heart transformation that must take place in man's heart by God's work alone. He was pointing to man's need for salvation by showing his absolute inability to fulfill these commands.

The Pharisees should have recognized their utter impotence to fulfill the law and cried out to God instead. Only as He has given us new hearts are believers able to exercise true love by the Spirit's enablement. The Pharisees had no heart change; they loved God and neighbor with no part of their hearts. They weren't even close. Likewise, moral people who try to treat people well haven't come *one* step closer to truly loving. *Unless you have been converted, you've not even begun to love.*

The Bible is clear: "Beloved, let us love one another, for *love is from God*; and *everyone who loves is born of God and knows God*" (1 John 4:7, emphases added). The neighborly love we are to bestow on our fellow brethren and the outside world originates from God. We cannot muster it up on our own. Only those whose hearts have been renovated—who are born of God and know Him—can truly love.

This is hard to wrap our minds around. It's a little easier to grasp that unbelievers can't truly love God, but other people? They sacrifice, they give, they do nice things, they have warm affection and undying attachment in some cases—but it can't be biblical love. This is not a popular statement. I preached on this truth years ago as a youth pastor, and I had a line at the pulpit afterward. They told me, "You're wrong. Can't everyone love their neighbor?" But the answer is no—*no one can love their neighbor apart from Jesus Christ*. That's what makes love so unique. They may have echoes of love, as we discussed before, but it's not effective. It does not accomplish God's will, nor does it please Him since it's outside of Christ.

It is because of our righteous standing before God in Christ that we have the basis upon which to cry out to God for this heavenly love. Because He is the source of love, we are dependent on Him for it. Through the truth of His Word and by the power of His Spirit, God strengthens us to demonstrate this love by faith.

Love Is Relational

God is relational. Before He created humanity, the world, the universe, and even time itself, the triune Godhead was enjoying perfect relationship. Made in His image, we are created as relational beings. It's part of our fundamental makeup. We have been fashioned to relate to God and one another.

Our sin forged an unbreachable chasm between us and God; nevertheless, He still has a relationship with every single person.

The rebellious, unrepentant sinner's relationship with God is fully hostile and belligerent—he is at enmity with His maker (Rom. 8:7), but he still relates to Him, nonetheless. As we discussed in chapter 4, the outcome of eternal life is to know Him and His Son in a reconciled, loving relationship (John 17:3).

Likewise, each one of us has some form of relationship with every other person in the world. We relate to everyone in varying ways and on varying levels. This may be hard for us to grasp. When we typically speak of relationships, we think of family members, significant others, friends, and coworkers. No doubt, these are our closest relationships, but we inherently relate to everyone. People are not simply objects. God does not view humanity this way and neither should we. Even though it's expressed in different ways, He loves the whole world (John 3:16).

We are called to do the same—to develop the deepest and most loving relationship as is biblically appropriate and possible with each person at any given moment. Only a few minutes may be afforded to relate to someone, but that doesn't mean it can't be truly loving. Witnessing to the man on the street inherently precludes an intimate relationship grown over time, and yet we can compassionately relate to him in those few moments and afterward as he comes to mind.

This is possible because our love for him should already be there. We must desire and seek to be in joyful, right relationship with everyone. *The goal is continual and intentional consideration of people in a relational manner. The Christian life is the relational life.* The total sum of our ministry in the church is defined by our relations with God and others as we seek to serve. While our first areas of responsibility are to love God and our fellow brethren, we are still called to relate well to those outside the church.

After addressing how believers should relate well with those in the body in Romans 12, Paul then addressed our relations with militant outsiders:

Bless those who persecute you; bless and do not curse. . . . Never pay back evil for evil to anyone. Respect what is right in the sight of all men. If possible, so far as it depends on you, be at peace with all men. Never take your own revenge, beloved, but leave room for the wrath of God, for it is written, "Vengeance is Mine, I will repay," says the Lord. "But if your enemy is hungry, feed him, and if he is thirsty, give him a drink, for in so doing you will heap burning goals on his head." Do not be overcome by evil, but overcome evil with good. (Rom. 12:14, 17–21)

With these principles of relating in mind, how well are you doing on social media, for example? Are you purposing to be at peace with all men? Or are you firing out caustic barbs to "own" your opponents? Even though digital screens separate the interaction, it's still relational. It's still personal.

Does the tone and tenor of your online presence primarily and predominantly reflect Christ—the most treasured relationship of all? Does your behavior in "real" life reveal an overarching desire for others to enjoy this supreme relationship? What a shame if, like the rest of the world, your online presence was just all about you. How does the self-promotion that social media facilitates communicate love for your neighbor? Everything we decide and do should be informed by our love for God and our neighbors.

Some of us check Christ at the business door, as if this area of life operates by another set of principles. We should biblically delight in relationships in this arena as well. Like Chick-fil-A's popular catchphrase, it should truly be our pleasure. Even to those who seek our downfall—in business or elsewhere—it can be our delight to demonstrate Christ to them. That is how we display Christlike love toward them—not brandishing our fists in anger as we clamor for our rights.

Sadly, we fail to delight in even our closest relationships as well. In marital or familial relationships, we can become embittered toward one another, using each other for our own ends. Or we can simply become used to one another. We operate in the same home, but it just becomes functional—we're not exerting the effort to delight in one another. Maybe we accomplish things in life, but we forget why God has us there in the first place—to intentionally and rightly relate to Him and one another.

Love Is Selfless and Humble

Many people readily admit they tend to be people-pleasers in their relationships. What they often don't realize is that the people-pleaser is, in reality, the self-pleaser. He seeks to please others so they will think well of him. Rather than a fault of being "too" selfless, people-pleasing is self-directed, self-promoting, self-exalting, and just plain selfish. At its root lays pride. Pride does not love others but desires to be *beloved* by others. It fights against biblical love which flourishes in the environs of humility.

Biblical love seeks the benefit of others as God defines it. Jesus was always perfectly loving; this included the firestorm He would shortly unleash on the Pharisees in our narrative (Matt. 23). Christ exemplified love in seeking even His enemies' highest good, regardless of what He received in return—in His case, death! Even from the cross He continued to love them. While the Roman executioners crucified Him, He cried out to His Father to forgive them (Luke 23:34). Such behavior reveals a humble, selfless heart.

Our own love shouldn't be focused on us and our needs. Biblical love that esteems others is not limiting but liberating! It should completely change our mindset, attitude, and perspective on every relationship—every act of relating—that we experience. We are freed up from the heavy burden of expecting to receive what we want in return. We don't have to deal with the resultant anger, despair, or bitterness when our "love" fails to be reciprocated in the manner we want—or at all!

Love Is Obedient to Scripture

As discussed in chapter 4, love is more than obedience, but it's never less. It's the driving force behind rightly motivated submission to what God's Word says. While obedience is directed toward God, it still pivotally impacts our neighbor. To the extent I am failing to keep God's commands, I am unloving toward my neighbor. Our measure of maturity, holiness, Christlikeness, growth, sanctification—however you wish to call it—affects others.

When we sin, whether it's directed at another or not, our love to God is not properly expressed. And when our love to God is not properly expressed, we cannot love each other well. This adds an entirely new motivation to pursuing holiness. Don't fool yourself. Don't think you can secretly dabble with pornography; or engage in cutthroat, unethical business dealings; or talk harshly and coldly to your wife in private, and then come to church and profess, "I love you." At the very least, you're not loving like you should. We cut off our ability to love others well when we disobey Scripture.

Our love to God drives us to know Him and understand what pleases Him—that which is in accordance with His character. Jesus clearly stated, "If you love Me, you will keep My commandments" (John 14:15). This pursuit of holiness is not some rigid, unforgiving, legalistic structure of self-righteous attainment. Ridiculous! *Holiness is love.*

John MacArthur published a book in the nineties entitled *The Love of God.* The subtitle was striking: *He Will Do Whatever It Takes to Make Us Holy.* That's what love means. It begins with God. He will do—He did do—everything necessary to conform us to the image of His Son. We are to love others in the same manner—pursuing everything necessary to see them transformed into Christ's likeness (more on that later). They don't get to define what love to them looks like any more than we do. We love others by doing what Scripture says. Love, therefore, can never say, "Oh, I would do anything for you." Love isn't heightened by such an expression but diminished by it.

Many of Scripture's commands deal explicitly with human relationships, particularly those in the church body. If we are not obeying God's Word in forgiving others and bearing with them; practicing patience and being at peace with them; rejoicing and weeping with them; honoring and serving them; carrying their burdens and confessing to them; demonstrating kindness and compassion to them; speaking truth graciously to them; confronting and admonishing them; submitting to, considering, and encouraging them, how are we loving our neighbor?

When Jesus declared Himself to be the true vine, He revealed: "Just as the Father has loved Me, I have also loved you; abide in My love. If you keep My commandments, you will abide in My love; just as I have kept My Father's commandments and abide in His love" (John 15:7–10). We abide in Christ's love when we keep His commandments, and the framework upon which His commandments are built is the love that reflects His character and nature. Abiding in Him and His Word means that we are obeying Him. This obedience begins with every thought, motivation, and affection and flows out into every decision, attitude, and behavior. That's love! It's exactly what Jesus did with His Father's Word that was embedded in His own heart and expressed outwardly toward us—fully obeying His Father every moment, all for the purpose of bringing Him glory. That was love, and He is our ultimate pattern.

While we noted the overt "One Another" commands, others may involve a complex application of multiple, implicit, biblical principles. Much wisdom is needed to accomplish this in our daily lives. The motivation of love is the same. The timeless truths of Scripture are the same. But how we experientially apply these truths in multifaceted and multitiered relationships differs. God's Spirit gives this wisdom through a proper understanding of the

truth in Scripture to live out what's best. That's why Paul wrote
to the Philippians,

> And this I pray, that your love may abound still more
> and more in real knowledge and all discernment, so
> that you may approve the things that are excellent,
> in order to be sincere and blameless until the day
> of Christ; having been filled with the fruit of
> righteousness which comes through Jesus Christ,
> to the glory and praise of God. (Phil. 1:9–11)

So how do we know "what's best" for our neighbor? Let's
tackle that in the next chapter.

CHAPTER 9

In Charles Dickens' classic *Little Dorrit*, one of the main protagonists is a kindly and respectable gentleman named Arthur Clennam. Arthur tirelessly and admirably labors to free a man languishing in a debtor's prison whom he believed his own family had wronged in the past. The story takes an ironic turn when, after securing the release of his friend, Arthur himself winds up a resident in the same prison following the collapse of a bank with whom he had invested all his business' capital.

His well-meaning but simple-minded friends Mr. & Mrs. Plornish come to visit Arthur to console him. Plornish attempts to cheer up Arthur by observing that life is full of ups and downs. Just as the world spins around, he argued, every man must take his turn on the bottom—upside down and hair "flying the wrong way." But just as inevitable, Plornish assured, was his turn to come back on top again, with his hair "a pleasure to look upon being all smooth again."[1]

---

1 Charles Dickens, *Little Dorrit* (London: Bradbury & Evans, 1857), full text accessible through the Gutenberg Project, https://www.gutenberg.org/files/963/963-h/963-h.htm.

While Plornish's folksy reasoning sounds absurd, the world's answers to life's pain and suffering are not much better. The culture can say, "Everything will turn out okay," or ,"It's going to be all right," but will it? Does it? What does that even look like? How do they know? They can only offer empty platitudes along with myriad distractions and ways to ignore or deaden the pain.

I've heard professing Christians confidently declare to others, "God works all things for good." While He does indeed, we must understand the context of this truth. In case you're wondering what this has to do with love, bear with me as we'll soon tie it together.

The Greater Good

Writing to the Christians in Rome, Paul addressed the "sufferings of this present time" (Rom. 8:18). Aside from the internal war waged against their own remaining sin (Rom. 7:4–8:17), these believers were beginning to experience the pangs of persecution for their faith, nested within other hardships such as slavery.

He comforted them with glorious truths in light of eternity in the subsequent verses (8:18–27). Then, he gave them a promise from God—He will cause everything, *all things*, good or bad, "to work together for good" (v. 28). While God places no restrictions on the trials included, He does place a qualifier on the recipients. His pledge of guaranteed and ultimate good is only reserved for "those who love God, to those who are called according to His purpose" (v. 28)—in short, for believers. An unbeliever should *never* be comforted with this verse because unless he repents, things will not work out for his ultimate good—quite the contrary, in fact.

What is the good He promised? What's the purpose to which He called them? At the very least, it can't mean that their trials would come to an abrupt end. We know that didn't happen. Many were martyrs for their faith. Paul defined their "good" in the next verse: "For those whom He foreknew, He also predestined to become *conformed to the image of His Son*" (v. 29, emphasis added).

This is the one thing we were meant to be—*Christlike*. We were saved and are sanctified to look like Jesus, "so that He would be the firstborn among many brethren" (v. 29). When we look like Christ, He is exalted, and the Father is glorified. What higher goal or good ought we to have?

Love is Helping Others Look like Jesus

We touched on this in the last chapter, but let's dig deeper. This is the highest good for every single person. It's the highest good for your neighbor. *The most loving thing we can do for our neighbors is to help them look like Jesus.* Since only believers are empowered and enabled to look like Him, the most loving thing to do for an unbeliever is to share the gospel with him. We faithfully proclaim the good news with the hope that he would come to know Christ—so that he could look like Him.

We help others look like Jesus by looking more like Him ourselves. Our imitation of Him demonstrates His worthiness. Imitation is not the "sincerest form of flattery," as the saying goes. It's the highest form of worship. In the last chapter, we worked halfway through our definition of love to neighbor: *The Holy Spirit-empowered affection and motivation to delight in relationship with others, which causes us to humbly obey every command of Scripture.* We concluded the chapter by asking: What is our neighbor's best? Now, we're considering the latter half: . . . *so that they would be continually conformed to the image of Christ, regardless of the sacrifice necessary and without any thought of what we might receive in return.*

It's insufficient to just say that loving others is doing their highest good—because who gets to determine that? We may decide that meeting the basic physical needs of others is the best thing for them, for example. Others may think it's expressing affection toward everyone to the highest degree possible for them to feel valued and accepted. But anybody can do either of those. That's not *biblical* love. Biblical love dictates that a person's greatest good at every moment is to look like Christ. Therefore, when I feed the hungry, for instance, my motivation for doing so is informed by the end goal of seeing them spiritually transformed.

This ties into the scriptural obedience from our definition. I extend forgiveness to my fellow brother in Christ; I show him compassion, admonish him, and more because I want him to look more like Jesus. If I want him to display Christlikeness, then "so far as it depends on [me]" (Rom. 12:18), I interact with him in such a way that makes it difficult for him to sin and easy for him to exercise holiness. Too often, the opposite happens. Through our own selfishness and pride, we practically roll out the red carpet for others to sin against us.

There are other layers added to our various expressions of love within relationships of varying intimacy, but it starts here. To take love and remove that underlying motivation shifts it into the subjective realm in which *we* define our own best apart from being transformed into Christ's character and nature.

We must keep this motivation at the forefront of our minds. When forgotten, our love slowly begins to turn worldly. Our spiritual fruit rots. It redirects inwardly and fades into a selfish, fleshly "love" that is conditional, weak, and inconstant. How often do we lose sight of love's purpose in our Christian marriages and our parenting? We forget that we're married so that our spouse would look more like Jesus—and that our looking more like Jesus together would more effectively help others to do the same.

Are your daily interactions with your spouse informed by this truth? Or have you reverted to the natural default of getting what you want? Is your parenting driven more by the natural desire to have compliant children who minimally inconvenience us and maximally reflect us well in public, or by them knowing and looking like Christ? This superficial, transient "love" only lasts until our desires are thwarted—which is usually not very long. It looks just like how the world uses people as their own little idols for their own little ends.

Rather, we must long for God's glory. Because He is most glorified when He is honored and reflected, we must seek to pray for others—even and including our enemies—to come to know Him. Are you willing to do whatever it takes, scripturally speaking, for someone else to look like Jesus?

True love is Christ-centered. That's why we should never be confused by worldly echoes of philanthropic sacrifice and the man-centered welldoings of moral religiosity. That isn't the measure of love—Christ is. Those whose hearts are spiritually dead and outside of Christ cannot love Him, appreciate Him, direct their efforts toward Him, or please Him. Because He is the measure of love, they entirely miss the mark. We must remember that if we ever shift the understanding of what love is away from Christ as the exclusive center, purpose, and focus, we've woefully redefined love.

Come What May

Moving right along in our definition, we modify this pursuit of seeing others look like Jesus with the phrase, *regardless of the sacrifice necessary.* As we discussed in chapter 4, love is more than the sum of sacrificial actions. Paul proved this point by arguing that if someone gives away every single possession to the poor and even his own life for others, he gains absolutely nothing if devoid of biblical love (1 Cor. 13:3).

Rightly motivated sacrifice says, "I will give up everything for you, not 'just because'—but to see you look like Christ." It's what Jesus did for us. While He laid His life down for us in death (1 John 3:16,) we generally lay our lives down for others through how we live. While reiterating that love is *more* than sacrifice, we must remember that it's never less. We must never exploit this truth to excuse our unwillingness to give of our time, finances, energy, convenience, and more. Charles Spurgeon keenly observed:

Love and self-denial for the object loved, go hand-in-hand. If I profess to love a certain person, and yet will neither give my silver nor my gold to relieve his wants, nor in any way deny myself comfort or ease for his sake, such love is contemptible; it wears the name, but lacks the reality of love: true love must be measured by the degree to which the person loving will be willing to subject himself to crosses and losses, to sufferings and self-denials. After all, the value of a thing in the market is what a man will give for it, and you must estimate the value of a man's love by that which he is willing to give up for it.[2]

You Love Me and I'll Love You

We love others by seeking their transformation into Christ's image. We accomplish this not only through any sacrifice necessary but also *without any thought of what we might receive in return.* In this sense, love is unconditional. It is not based on the merit, worth, or response of the person loved. Clarification here is key, though. As always, this presumes scriptural boundaries. When the world describes love as "unconditional," it means unhitched from God's definition. They want wholesale acceptance and affirmation of everything they are and do.

Ironically, while the world enjoys touting their own love as unconditional, they constantly practice conditional, reciprocated love. Their love is often based on merit and the responses of others. Always silently evaluating what others have to offer in their hearts, they decide who deserves their good graces.

2   Charles H. Spurgeon, "Love's Crowning Deed," sermon, Metropolitan Tabernacle, London, August 23, 1873, transcript from Metropolitan Tabernacle Pulpit vol. 19, The Spurgeon Center, https://www.spurgeon.org/resource-library/sermons/loves-crowning-deed/#flipbook/.

Instead, Christians are called to freely give our love to the fullest extent at every moment. When it's unreciprocated, this in no way changes our mandate. Granted, the rejection of our love will prevent further growth in relationship with someone, but it should never change our heart's response to that person. We would certainly desire and pray that our biblical love expressed would draw another toward Christ—and ourselves as an outflow—but it's not required. Why? Because "while we were yet sinners, Christ died for us" (Rom. 5:8). Because "while we were enemies we were reconciled to God through the death of His Son" (5:10). No one must ever earn our love because we did not earn God's love.

Even though we may not say this, we sometimes live it. Our spouse may wrong us, and we feel as though he needs to be chastised with a little less love for a period of time. Perhaps our children go through a phase of responding well to us, and we find that our love increases toward them on that basis. Our love should never fluctuate, however. It should be full-bore, maximum strength love, all the time.

In writing to the churches in Asia Minor, Peter exhorted his readers to "fervently love one another from the heart" because their souls were purified "for a sincere love of the brethren" (1 Pet. 1:22). This love for the church was to be driven by a pure heart exercised deeply. Peter's Greek term for "fervently" meant "to stretch out." The picture was of "something stretched out and extended to the limit," such as a violin whose string "has been stretched to a tighter pitch that it might yield a little higher note," or of an athlete whose taut muscles strain under "strenuous and sustained effort."[3] This is no mere emotional warmth! This is the same word used to describe Christ as He "was praying very *fervently*; and His sweat became like drops of blood, falling down upon the ground (Luke 22:44, emphasis added).

We must emanate the sweet aroma of love poured out on others regardless of whether they have ever loved us in return a single time. This caliber of love will change our marriages, parenting, and every

---

3   D. Edmond Hiebert, *1 Peter* (Chicago: Moody Press, 1992), 113–114.

other relationship. By the Holy Spirit's empowerment through the truth of God's Word, He provides the necessary resources to make possible the exercise of this measure of love. Indeed, we turn to Scripture to see the One who supremely modeled this love for us perfectly.

Jesus, Lover of My Soul

Charles Spurgeon poignantly said of Christ's love:

> Why, if a man should want to know about slavery, he might go and hear a lecture by an escaped slave, and it would be very well for him to do so; but if he could go to the place where the whip is cracking, and the back is bleeding, and see the thing for himself, then he would understand the cruelty of slavery, indeed. So, if a man would know the love of Christ, he must lay himself out to discover the deformity of sin . . . and then he will know that love which stoops from the highest heaven can reach down to the gates of the deepest hell, and can thrust its arms up to the very elbows in the mire to pull these accursed ones out of the pit of destruction, and make them blessed for ever among the shining ones before the throne.[4]

Additionally, Walter Chantry once observed: "As Christ struggled up Calvary's hill and bled upon it, His aim was to eradicate self-love and implant the love of God in the hearts of

---

4 Charles H. Spurgeon, "The Love of Jesus," sermon, Metropolitan Tabernacle, London, June 18, 1862, transcript from Metropolitan Tabernacle Pulpit vol. 8, The Spurgeon Center, https://www.spurgeon.org/resource-library/sermons/the-love-of-jesus/#flipbook/. This site uses the term "distinction" in lieu of "destruction." Other transcriptions render the word "distraction." I opted for the term that seemed to fit the context best.

men. One can only increase as the other decreases."[5] In seeking to find the highest example of love, no mere human illustration will do. The matchless demonstration of God's love is on full display in the gospel of Jesus Christ. Perfect, unadulterated love isn't found by searching inwardly but by looking outwardly unto Him.

At the very beginning of this book, I laid out that *love cannot be found or understood apart from the character of God and the person and work of Jesus Christ as revealed in His Word*. I proposed that *Jesus Himself is the model for, and the foundation of, the love that forms the central motivation for all relationship and obedience in the Christian life*. His love successfully accomplished our salvation, but it also served as an example for us to imitate.

The Pharisaic lawyer's question that kicked off this whole discussion was posed to Jesus at the beginning of the week He would demonstrate this love to the highest degree on the cross. He performed many good works, such as healing and feeding the masses during His ministry, but He always had this primary purpose in mind.

Copycat Love

As mentioned earlier, Jesus quoted from Leviticus when citing the commandment to love our neighbor. Yet at the same time, Jesus said it's new: "A *new* commandment I give to you, that you love one another, even as I have loved you, that you also love one another" (John 13:34, emphasis added). What's that about? How is this a *new* commandment? He tells us in His own words—*"as I have loved you."* He gave us the pattern. We know exactly what it looks like now. With the incarnation, His disciples witnessed the very embodiment of God's love. Its content has been fully filled in.

Through the pages of Scripture, we learn how to follow Christ's example of loving others to the fullest. Similar to Jesus' call to love

5 Walter Chantry, *The Shadow of the Cross* (Carlisle, PA: Banner of Truth, 1981), 14.

like Him, Peter called believers—slaves, in particular—to suffer like Him as well, pointing out that He left "an example for [us] to follow in His steps" (1 Pet. 2:21). Peter used the Greek term *hupogrammon* for "example." Only used here in the Bible, this word literally meant "underwriting" and could refer to "a writing or drawing that was placed under another sheet to be retraced on the upper sheet by the pupil."[6] Sometimes the image or lettering to be copied was at the top of the page, but the student must still render a replica—"line by line, feature by feature." That's how tightly we must imitate Christ's love.

The apostle shifted metaphors a bit to exhort the recipients of his letter to follow in Jesus' steps. The picture was that we would place our feet exactly where His footprints were marked. Many years ago, I repeatedly attempted to climb a particular rock face in Colorado's Garden of the Gods to no avail. I found it not only difficult but impossible. Then I found a guy who knew how to do it. He led me up, talking me through the entire process as he showed me exactly how he did it. He instructed me to place my hand in specific spots at specific angles to build more pressure, place my foot on an almost invisible nub and smear into the rock to reach the next hold, and so forth. I did exactly what he told me and showed me, and I made it all the way up! I went from not even coming close, to successfully climbing it, all because of his example. This is the idea.

Effective Love

While Jesus exemplified love to the utmost, His love exercised on the cross was *much more* than just an example. His death on the cross was not merely an expression of affection for us, nor just an admirable illustration of self-sacrifice. He offered a substitutionary, wrath-bearing sacrifice by dying on the cross so that we would be reconciled, redeemed, and released from all condemnation.

6 Hiebert, *1 Peter*, 182–183.

Fulfilling love to neighbor to the highest degree, He died so we would look like Him. In other words, His love was effective. *All our love, in turn, must be grounded in and driven by Jesus' demonstration of love expressed through dying in the place of sinners.*

John stated: "We have come to know and have believed the love which God has for us. God is love, and the one who abides in love abides in God, and God abides in him" (1 John 4:16). He reminded us that love begins with God and that we appropriate it by faith. The love displayed on the cross was first and foremost Christ's love to God. In just a few short nights after the Pharisee's question, Jesus would pray, "Father, the hour has come; glorify Your Son, that the Son may glorify You" (John 17:1). Our definition of love to God primarily involves glorifying Him and that is exactly what Jesus does by obeying His Father's will.

The cross was also an expression of His love for us. In his gospel, John also shared that Jesus, "knowing that His hour had come [. . . and] loving His own who were in the world, He loved them to the end" (John 13:1). He loved His disciples—and by extension us—fervently, perfectly, and to the uttermost. *The cross was loving because it accomplished the purposes for which God intended it.* Contrary to modern Christian theology, it isn't only an incredible example of selfless devotion to others. It *is* that, but it's so much more. The Bible teaches that Christ's work was substitutionary and propitiatory in nature: "He loved us and sent His Son to be the propitiation for *our* sins" (1 John 4:10, emphasis added). If we remove this, we remove God's love. His love is always completely effective and achieves its end. The objective of the cross is what makes it truly loving. Strip this away, and love is also removed.

Jesus' love was rich with intentional purpose: He loved us to die our death, a substitutionary sacrifice (1 Pet. 3:18); He loved us to pay our price, a redemptive sacrifice (Col. 1:13–14); He loved us to bear our wrath, a propitiatory sacrifice (Rom. 3:24–25); He loved us to forgive our sins, a sin-bearing sacrifice (Heb. 9:22); He loved us to provide us life, a life-giving sacrifice (Rom. 6:23); He loved us to purchase our pardon, a justifying sacrifice (Gal. 2:16); He loved us to give us righteousness, a sanctifying sacrifice (2 Cor. 5:21); He loved us to bestow on us glory, a glory-giving sacrifice (John 17:22); and He loved us to bring us into relationship with Him, a relational sacrifice (John 17:3). Praise be to the King of kings and Lord of lords!

CHAPTER 10

I f the entire Bible could be boiled down to one word, *love* would take the top spot. While we typically think of God's love toward man, Jesus made clear that man's love toward God and others fulfills every single command in Scripture. This is radically life-changing, but it's only meaningful to the extent we understand and apply it. While the Bible may be distilled into this one word, *it takes the entire Bible to make that word meaningful.* Like we said in chapter 7, content matters. Once we fill in the proper understanding of love, we must believe and exercise it for God's greatness to be reflected. Thankfully, we can look to Jesus for the kind of love through which all the teaching of Scripture is fulfilled.

A Tuesday to Remember

Did you know Tuesdays are considered the most productive day of the week?[1] Or that the Anglo-Saxons exchanged the Roman god

---

1 Tom R. Skattenborg, "Why is Tuesday the Most Productive Day of the Week?" *The Flexible Professional*, November 8, 2020, https://theflexibleprofessional. com/why-is-tuesday-the-most-productive-day-of-the-week/.

Mars for *Tiu*, the Germanic god of war, as their namesake for the week's third day?[2] A handful of notable events in history occurred on Tuesdays, including D-Day, the Allied invasion of Normandy during WWII, and 9/11, the terrorist attacks on American soil in 2001 that toppled the World Trade Center.

In Judaism, Tuesdays are considered lucky because it was the only day of the week recorded in Genesis that God twice reflected that "it was good."[3] If the Jewish leaders of Jesus' day held to that belief, they must have been doubting it on the Tuesday of Passion Week. Every attempt to trip Him up had failed. He silenced every challenge made to His authority. Little did they know that right after Jesus responded to this last question, they would receive the condemnation of a lifetime in the barrage of "woe's" Jesus would soon release.

His denunciation of them was fundamentally bound up in one thing—they refused to love Him. They didn't love Him because they didn't truly love God. They rejected Him because they truly rejected God. Earlier in His ministry, Jesus pointed out to them that while they searched the Scripture, they hated God: "[B]ut I know you, that you do not have the love of God in yourselves. I have come in My Father's name, and you do not receive Me" (John 5:42–43). He rebuked them on another occasion, claiming, "If God were your Father, you would love Me, for I proceeded forth and have come from God" (John 8:42). He implied that they hated Him despite their endless repetitions of the Shema.

The Pharisees were really asking, "What's the one thing we need to know above all else?" Jesus told them to love the Lord their God and love their neighbor. This is what the world needs to hear as well, but too often it's used as a cliché that's devoid of the right content. Our world stands in their spot today. Their claims

---

2 "Tuesday is Named for a One-handed God Named Tiu," Dictionary.com, April 22, 2014, https://www.dictionary.com/e/tuesday/.
3 Wikipedia, s.v. "Tuesday," last modified May 8, 2023, 10:17, https://en.wikipedia.org/wiki/Tuesday.

to love fall short because unregenerate man neither understands the Word nor knows God.

Both of our definitions of love in this book are based on what God's Word reveals. We need to know precisely what love is—backwards and forwards—to successfully and effectively live out the one thing God calls us to do.

Love Fulfills the Law

After Jesus answered the lawyer, He concluded, "On these two commandments depend the whole Law and the Prophets" (Matt. 22:40). This is a powerful, comprehensive statement. His phrase, "the whole Law and the Prophets," referred to the entire Old Testament—every command and principle it contained. From Genesis to Malachi, Jesus included everything.

What did Jesus mean by Scripture *depending* entirely on these two related points? The verb He selected is much more intense than our English word. The Greek term meant to "physically hang."[4] In a visceral example, the word was used to describe the crucified body strung up on a cross. The idea was that all of one's weight was fully suspended on the structure in question. In just a few days, Jesus would demonstrate this verb with His own body.

Likewise, He meant that the entire weight of the law of God rested on the foundation of these two core truths. Our one-word summary of the Bible was no exaggeration—everything depends on love to God first and foremost and to others as an outflow. Paul says it this way to the Galatians: "For the whole Law is fulfilled in one word, in the statement, "You shall love your neighbor as yourself." (Gal. 5:14).

Notice that Jesus did *not* say love replaced, annulled, or in any way abolished the law. Rather, He said the law hangs on love. It is fulfilled by it. Jesus is providing a "'hermeneutic program' for

---

4 Strong's Concordance, G2910, s.v. "*kremannymi*," Blue Letter Bible, https://www.blueletterbible.org/lexicon/g2910/nasb95/mgnt/0-1/.

the understanding and application of the law and the prophets."[5] He revealed that the underlying principle behind these two commandments is the lens through which to understand God's entire law. R. T. France agreed:

> The two texts chosen by Jesus are together sufficiently strong to bear the weight of the whole OT. This does not mean, as some modern ethicists have argued, that "all you need is love," so that one can dispense with the ethical rules set out in the Torah. It is rather to say that those rules find their true role in working out the practical implications of the love for God and neighbor on which they are based. Far from making the law irrelevant, therefore, love thus becomes "the primary hermeneutical principle for interpreting and applying the law."[6]

Hermeneutics is a fancy word for the methodological principles of interpreting Scripture. A grammatical-historical hermeneutic, for example, is an approach to scriptural interpretation that seeks to discover the author's intention to the specific audience for whom he is writing. Similarly, Jesus is teaching that these two greatest commandments encompass every other command, so the entire law should be viewed in light of them. The New Testament repeatedly testifies to Jesus' instruction.

An Unpayable Debt

Returning to the Charles Dickens' novel, we find our protagonist—the honorable Arthur Clennam—languishing in the debtor's prison after freeing his friend. He anticipates the dreadful meeting with his business partner returning from ventures abroad. He would have to break the awful news to him that he lost all their money with the collapsed banking scandal. Daniel Doyce, however, wouldn't hear any of it. The business was prospering and growing so rapidly, the debts were already paid in full. Daniel enthusiastically related to Arthur that he could leave the prison almost at once and return to the company's helm.[7]

We all love a good story of a debt fully paid, but Paul tells the Roman church about a debt that can never, ever be paid off:

> Owe nothing to anyone except to love one another; for he who loves his neighbor has fulfilled the law. For this, "YOU SHALL NOT COMMIT ADULTERY, YOU SHALL NOT MURDER, YOU SHALL NOT STEAL, YOU SHALL NOT COVET," and if there is any other commandment, it is summed up in this saying, "YOU SHALL LOVE YOUR NEIGHBOR AS YOURSELF." Love does no wrong to a neighbor; therefore love is the fulfillment of the law. (Rom. 13:8–10)

Like Jesus, Paul taught that *love is our primary obligation*. He had just finished instructing these believers to "[r]ender to all what is due them: tax to whom tax is due; custom to whom custom; fear to whom fear; honor to whom honor" (Rom. 13:7). Debts must always be fully paid, even though some take a little longer than others. But the apostle revealed the *one* debt that will always remain for the rest of our lives and even into eternity—love.

There will never be a time when the debt is paid off in full. You can never tell another person, "My obligation to love you is finished." Love is continually owed. This understanding is at cross-purposes with our evaluation of loving others. We tend to think we are doing others a favor by loving them biblically. This can breed thinking that others actually owe us! But the Bible teaches the opposite. We owe everyone in the world the fullness

---

7 Dickens, *Little Dorrit*.

of our love all the time. They don't have to earn it. They don't have to deserve it. Jesus said, "[W]hen you do all the things which are commanded you, say, 'We are unworthy slaves; we have done only that which we ought to have done'" (Luke 17:10).

When we are tempted to be unloving to others, we must recall our debt to them. The early church father Origen explained that "we should both pay this debt daily and always owe it."[8] Thankfully, there's an infinite supply of love from God upon which we can draw and dispense to those around us. By fully paying our sin debt, Jesus gifts us with this debt of love in its place.

Love Motivates and Empowers

Love provides us with the motivation and power to obey God's commands that reflect His nature. When biblical love drives our desires, thinking, and behavior, we can fully and truly obey God. Otherwise, we would be externally obeying, like the Pharisees, but fail to actually *fulfill* the law. Paul knew this better than anyone. A "Hebrew of Hebrews," the apostle described himself as blameless according to the Law when he was an unbeliever (Phil. 3:4–6). But the law's requirement went unfulfilled because his heart attitude was wrong—it wasn't driven by a desire for others to look like the Messiah.

We have been using the term "law" as often as Jesus and Paul, but what do we mean? Generally speaking, the law is the commandments and principles that His Word lays out for us to obey. It has been expressed differently throughout history. In the Old Testament, the law could refer to the Mosaic Law as a whole, or just the Ten Commandments, sacrificial laws, ceremonial laws, or the civil laws created for God's chosen nation Israel as they lived underneath His rulership. Those who lived under these forms of the

---

8 C.E.B. Cranfield, *A Critical and Exegetical Commentary on the Epistle to the Romans*, vol. 2:9-16 (New York: T & T Clark, 2004), 674. Cranfield is quoting Origen.

law—even commands that appeared to be amoral or external—were expected to obey from a regenerated heart properly motivated by love to God and others.

Now, we live under the new covenant, or the law of Christ, as Paul called it—that is, every command that continues to express God's character and nature. For the time in which we now live, the intent of God's moral law is the same as it has always been—*to bring glory and honor to God through a right relationship with Him and others through conformity to His character and nature as expressed in His commands.* The church is to obey Christ's law from the heart as well, and God has graciously gifted us with the permanent indwelling of the Holy Spirit. At any point in human history, the power and motivation to obey any aspect of God's law must come from love. This is why love doesn't replace the law but fulfills it.

Love In Deed

The law gives legs to love. Love's actions are defined by God's commands. It's what love looks like and how it's expressed. In our Romans passage, Paul gave some examples from the Ten Commandments. Love doesn't commit adultery or murder, neither does it steal or covet. He covers every other command by including them under the umbrella of Jesus' second greatest commandment. Professor Thomas Schreiner comments:

> All the various commands of the law are simply expressions of love. Love is the heart and soul of the commands, so that if one begins to focus on the commands and loses sight of love, then rigidity . . . and legalism are sure to follow. Indeed, there are countless situations in life in which no [explicit] law can be formulated to specify what is exactly the right course of action (though there are principles for "everything pertaining to life and godliness" (2

Pet. 1:3)). Believers need to pray in these situations that their love will abound and that this love will be conjoined with wisdom so that they will choose the right course.[2] (brackets and parentheses added)

Let's look at Paul's examples in light of love: Adultery is love perverted—using another to satisfy one's own lust. Murder is love abused—taking another's life rather than giving one's own. Stealing is love trampled—taking from others rather than sacrificing to give to them. Coveting is love twisted—desiring the stuff of others rather than seeking the best for others.

This works for every relational command in Scripture—for the ones that only His chosen people were called to obey and the moral commands the church must come underneath. Go through your Bible and try this exercise. Your inner man needs to be informed by this love so that you're properly motivated. God's commands flesh out what it looks like to love someone. This is how Paul can say, "Bear one another's burdens (in love), and thereby fulfill the law of Christ" (Gal. 6:2, parentheses added).

Paul continued, "Love does no wrong to a neighbor; therefore love is the fulfillment of the law" (Rom. 13:10). He is simply flipping the positive truth that love always seeks what is best over to the negative side. It is appropriate to conclude, then, *love always does right to a neighbor*. Behind every violation of the law—every sin, every transgression—is always a lack of love. Jesus' brother James pointed this out to those who were practicing the sin of partiality toward their fellow brethren. He said to those resisting such a temptation, "If, however, you are fulfilling the royal law according to the Scripture, 'YOU SHALL LOVE YOUR NEIGHBOR AS YOURSELF,' you are doing well" (Jam. 2:8).

Perhaps you've been wondering why Paul says that the command Jesus ranked second is the fulfillment of the law. Why not the first?

9 Thomas Schreiner, *Baker Exegetical Commentary on the New Testament: Romans*, vol. 6 (Grand Rapids: Baker Academic, 1998), 692.

Why isn't loving God with your entire being the law's fulfillment? While he's specifically focused on love for others, I think it goes deeper than that. As we learned, the two are so inextricably linked, love for others is how our love for God is predominantly expressed in practice. John couldn't be clearer:

> If someone says, "I love God," and hates his brother, he is a liar; for the one who does not love his brother whom he has seen, cannot love God whom he has not seen. And this commandment we have from Him, that the one who loves God should love his brother also. (1 John 4:20–21)

Love to others, then, becomes a kind of scriptural litmus test as to whether or not we're actually loving God. It's the evidence for others to know we truly love Him when we profess it.

Jesus gave a very similar line of reasoning when He healed a paralyzed man. Teaching in a packed house that included some Scribes and Pharisees, Jesus observed the paralytic's faith and informed the man, "Son, your sins are forgiven" (Mark 2:5). Fulfilling the man's greatest need—to be healed of his spiritual disease—was the most loving thing Jesus could do. The religious leaders inwardly shuddered, angry at such blasphemy for making a proclamation that only God could issue.

Demonstrating omniscience to boot, Jesus questioned them, "Which is easier, to say to the paralytic, 'Your sins are forgiven'; or to say, 'Get up, and pick up your pallet and walk'?" (2:9). They would've surmised that it's much easier to just say your sins are forgiven. Anybody could say that. How would they know if it actually happened? In their eyes, the harder task was miraculously healing a lame man. Who could pull that off? In reality, if Christ could actually pardon a sinner and save his eternal soul, this is a much greater feat than restoring the use of his temporal, physical limbs.

Mark records Jesus' infinite wisdom: "'But so that you may know that the Son of Man has authority on earth to forgive sins'—He said to the paralytic, 'I say to you, get up, pick up your pallet and go home.' And he got up and immediately picked up the pallet and went out in the sight of everyone" (2:10–12). So that they know the weightier portion that's unseen is true, here was the evidence. In the same way, our love for others is to be evidence of our ultimate love for God above all else. How would you measure up on this litmus test? We must always strive to love more—greater, deeper, stronger, further.

While the law is meant to be a tool of judgment and condemnation to the unbelieving sinner who's incapable of keeping it, it becomes a gracious blessing to His Spirit-empowered children to teach them how to specifically love others wisely and well.

CHAPTER 11

Have you ever played "Would You Rather"? It's a fun conversational game to break the ice at dinner parties. The questions tend to reveal the personality of the one who must choose between two options. Sometimes it's a selection based on the lesser of two evils: Would you rather lose your sight or your memories? Labor under a hot sun or extreme cold? Spend a year at war or in prison? Give up your phone or bathing? Other times, thankfully, it's a choice between good and better: Would you rather see ten minutes into the future or 150 years? Have telekinesis or telepathy? Have a personal maid or a personal chef? Run 100 mph or fly 20 mph?

God's progressive revelation throughout history works in a similar manner. While we have made clear that the old covenant had fully sufficient revelation for true saints to obey from a heart of love, the law itself was not necessarily designed to save. Rather, it pointed toward the new covenant to come when the law would flow through the person and work of Christ. The new covenant would fill out the ability to biblically love to the fullest degree.

Old Testament saints *could* love to the fullest according to their revelation and were commanded to do so. This was also accomplished by the Lord's grace, but New Testament saints have been blessed with a fuller, more complete understanding and thus a greater ability, in that sense, to love. That also means we have had a greater responsibility to love these past two thousand years. Let's consider some of those blessings.

The Blessing of Christ

As we already laid out, Christ came to reveal the character and nature of God. His life is our prime pattern to follow. While the believers from the Old Testament could only look forward to their coming Messiah, Deliverer, Redeemer, and King, we have the Apostles' accounts of "the Word" who "became flesh, and dwelt among [them], and [they] saw His glory, glory as of the only begotten from the Father, full of grace and truth" (John 1:14).

Paul made a case for his "Would You Rather" choice by comparing these two time periods, referring to them as "ministries":

> But if the ministry of death, in letters engraved on stones, came with glory, so that the sons of Israel could not look intently at the face of Moses because of the glory of his face, fading as it was, how will the ministry of the Spirit fail to be even more with glory? For if the ministry of condemnation has glory, much more does the ministry of righteousness abound in glory. . . . But to this day whenever Moses is read, a veil lies over their heart; but whenever a person turns to the Lord, the veil is taken away. Now the Lord is the Spirit, and where the Spirit of the Lord is, there is liberty. But we all, with unveiled face, beholding as in a mirror the glory of the Lord, are being transformed into the same

image from glory to glory, just as from the Lord, the Spirit. (2 Cor. 3:7–9; 15–18)

Although we did not see Him ourselves, we have His person revealed to us, in word and deed, along with the work He accomplished.

From this side of the cross, we have His atoning death that already took place and was recorded for us in His Word. Whereas the old covenant had the sacrificial system, we have the once-for-all, perfect sacrifice. The author of Hebrews makes a comparison as well: "Every priest stands daily ministering and offering time after time the same sacrifices, which can never take away sins; but [Jesus], having offered one sacrifice for sins for all time, SAT DOWN AT THE RIGHT HAND OF GOD" (Heb. 12:11–12, brackets added). What a blessing!

The Blessing of the Spirit

While the Holy Spirit was active in the old covenant, He only indwelled a few people for certain tasks and for a limited time. He still regenerated Old Testament saints, bringing them from spiritual death to spiritual life, but for new covenant believers after Pentecost, we are blessed with the Holy Spirit's immediate and permanent indwelling within our inner man. In this sense, there is no further need for a physical temple of God in Jerusalem.

We are empowered by the Spirit to live out the Christian walk, including biblical love. This is how Jesus was able to say: "But I tell you the truth, it is to your advantage that I go away; for if I do not go away, the Helper will not come to you; but if I go, I will send Him to you. . . . [W]hen He, the Spirit of truth, comes, He will guide you into all the truth" (John 16:7, 13).

The Blessing of the Word

God graciously ordained to reveal Himself in progressive stages to humanity throughout history, culminating in the revelation of His own Son. After He laid the foundation of the church with the Apostles, God concluded this disclosure with His last disciple on the island of Patmos. Scripture is now complete, wholly inerrant and infallible, and fully sufficient. As a result, for the last two millennia, the church has been blessed with the full revelation of God.

The New Testament—which was not written yet when Jesus answered the Pharisaic lawyer—sheds even more light on His response. The gospels testify to Jesus' own demonstration of love; the book of Acts records the manifestations of love among the brethren in the early church; Paul's epistles and the other letters further flesh out how to properly love; and the last book prophesies of the love-drenched marriage supper of the Lamb (Christ) and His Bride (the church).

Through this half of the Bible, we are taught that everything we do should "be done in love" (1 Cor. 16:14). Jesus made clear that if we love Him, we must keep His commands (John 14:15). He repeatedly reminded the disciples, "This is My commandment, that you love one another, just as I have loved you" (John 15:12); not only each other but our enemies (Matt. 5:44).

John recalled his Lord's words. Writing to the church, he informed them that Jesus' instruction was to believe in Him and "love one another, just as He commanded us" (1 John 3:23). Over and over, he assured them that "this is the message which you have heard from the beginning, that we should love one another" (1 John 3:11). He encouraged all of us that "if we love one another, God abides in us, and His love is perfected in us" (1 John 4:12). He explained that perfect love "casts out fear, because fear involves punishment, and the one who fears is not perfected in love" (1 John 4:18). He even gently admonished the female recipient of his second letter: "Now I ask you, lady, not as though I were writing to you a new commandment, but the one which we have had from the beginning, that we love one another. And this is love, that we walk according to His commandments" (2 John 5–6).

Pointing out the practical aspect of love, Peter exhorted the believers scattered across ancient Turkey to "above all, keep fervent in [their] love for one another, because love covers a multitude of sins" (1 Pet. 4:8). The author of Hebrews also focused on the functional aspect of love by urging his hearers to "consider how to stimulate one another to love and good deeds, not forsaking [their] own assembling together, as is the habit of some, but encouraging one another; and all the more as [they] see the day drawing near" (Heb. 10:24–25).

Paul fleshed out love in great detail to the Corinthians. He described love as patient, kind, selfless, humble, modest, unprovoked, forgiving, pure, true, forbearing, believing, hoping, enduring, and unfailing (1 Cor. 13:4–7). He then compared love to faith and hope, both of which will not be necessary in eternity, Paul declared that "the greatest of these is love" (1 Cor. 13:13).

He commanded the Galatian church, "[T]hrough love serve one another" (Gal. 5:13). He told the Roman church to be "devoted to one another in brotherly love" (Rom. 12:10), the Philippian church to "[d]o nothing from selfishness or empty conceit, but with humility of mind [to] regard one another as more important than [themselves]" (Phil. 2:3), and the Ephesian church to show "tolerance for one another in love" (Eph. 4:2). Paul admonished the Corinthians, "Let no one seek his own good, but that of his neighbor" (1 Cor. 10:24), and, "Let all that you do be done in love" (16:14). He even wrote to the Thessalonian church "concerning brotherly love," that they had "no need for anyone to write to [them], for [they themselves were] taught by God to love one another" (1 Thess. 4:9); but that didn't keep him from praying for the Lord to cause them to "increase and abound in love for one another, and for all people" (1 Thess. 3:12).

Lastly, the New Testament sheds light on love expressed in familial relationships. Paul instructed Titus to ensure older women were encouraging "the younger women to love their husbands" and their children (Tit. 2:4). But he gave a very detailed command for husbands to love their wives. The comparison on which he drew to illustrate the nature of this love gives valuable insight into Christ's relationship with His church. He exhorted them to love their wives

> just as Christ also loved the church and gave Himself up for her, so that He might sanctify her, having cleansed her by the washing of water with the word, that He might present to Himself the church in all her glory, having no spot or wrinkle or any such thing; but that she would be holy and blameless. (Eph. 5:25–27)

Like Jesus' point of loving our neighbor in the way we naturally care for ourselves, Paul concluded that each husband "is to love his own wife even as himself" (Eph. 5:33).

The Blessing of the Church

Last but not least, we have been blessed with the only institution on earth God is actively growing and building—the church, Christ's own bride. Nothing will hinder its growth, and "the gates of Hades will not overpower it" (Matt. 16:18). While we all comprise the universal church, our love is chiefly demonstrated within the local body of believers. Practically speaking, the local church, underneath biblically qualified leadership, is where the "one anothers" of Scripture take place. God uses the fellowship of believers in a local body to strengthen, encourage, and grow us "until we all attain to the unity of the faith, and of the knowledge of the Son of God, to a mature man, to the measure of the stature which belongs to the fullness of Christ" (Eph. 4:13).

Sadly, Christians do not often grasp the utmost importance of the local body when it comes to love. We can't fully love without it. It is essential that we are an active member of a local, biblically sound, healthy church under which we can submit to the leadership and pursue unity as we build others up through our unique spiritual giftings. The relationships within this body are foundational.

Paul's letter to the Colossians provides some wisdom on this topic:

> So, as those who have been chosen of God, holy and beloved, put on a heart of compassion, kindness, humility, gentleness and patience; bearing with one another, and forgiving each other, whoever has a complaint against anyone; just as the Lord forgave you, so also should you. *Beyond all these things put on love, which is the perfect bond of unity.* (Col. 3:12–14, emphasis added)

While we seek to put off all sin, we renew our minds with the truth of the Word. Because God has placed His love upon us, making us holy, we exercise this new heart He has given us—one that is empowered by the Spirit to bear all these choice fruits: compassion, kindness, humility, gentleness, patience, forbearance, and grace. You cannot exercise these virtues by yourself or on yourself! They are relational. Most of these qualities also imply that our spiritual brothers and sisters will be difficult and sinful at times. How can we be patient, for example, if no one is testing us? Extending forgiveness can be so great a challenge, Paul gives extra reasoning and motivation with biblical truths. Because Christ forgave us so much more, we should stand ready to forgive anyone.

Paul continued, "Beyond all these things put on love which is the perfect bond of unity" (v. 14). As we practice biblical love that helps others to look more like Jesus, we become more and more united. We were already "called in one hope of [our] calling; one Lord, one faith, one baptism, one God and Father of all who is over all and through all and in all" (Eph. 4:4–6), but we must still be "diligent to preserve the unity of the Spirit in the bond of peace" (Eph. 4:3). Love accomplishes this. Picture it as the glue that's poured down through the cracks and holds us all together. Earlier in Colossians, Paul described it as being "knit together in love" (Col. 2:2).

We are united to the extent we are loving well. We accomplish this through being "filled with the Spirit" by "let[ting] the word of Christ richly dwell within [us]" (Eph. 5:18; Col. 3:16). Remember, it's not just being nice. Friendly people in social clubs can exhibit a level of these listed virtues, but they will *never* be Christ-centered, Christ-focused, Christ-empowered, and Christ-exalting.

This love, then, extends out to the unbelieving world around us through the proclamation of the gospel. The Good News on our lips must be testified to by the way we love each other in the church. Jesus taught, "By this all men will know that you are My disciples, if you have love for one another" (John 13:35). It must be unlike anything the world has ever seen. In fact, it's the *only* thing the world will ever see of real love. There is no other group of people on the face of the earth who can do this. Only the church has this power.

Considering that reality, how are you handling the responsibility? Are you properly reflecting God's character and nature as expressed through His Word—first, back toward Him, then extending out to your church, and finally, the world as a whole?

I pray that you will treasure the Lord's response to the Pharisees on that Tuesday of Passion Week when asked about the greatest commandment. May you pursue loving God and neighbor with Spirit-empowered, reckless abandon. Build your life on this one thing, and you'll have no regrets.

QUESTIONS FOR REFLECTION

1. Reflecting on all that you read, is your life defined by a love for God? Or is it possible that your love for family, yourself, work, pleasure, politics, or something else is greater?

2. Is it your delight to know God? Why or why not?

3. Are you finding your satisfaction in God? In what ways?

4. Are you pursuing a knowledge of God? How?

5. Are you laying down your life for God? Name three ways in which you are already doing this. Name one new way you will lay your life down this week.

6. Is there anyone you are excluding in the definition of *neighbor* (and thus not loving)? What steps can you take to treat them as a neighbor?

7. Are you fooling yourself into thinking that you love others when your love is less than biblical? How can you change that?

8. How is your Christ-esteem? Your self-esteem? Your esteem of others? How are we to esteem ourselves and others?

9. Do you delight in relationship with others—even those who can't provide you any benefit in return? Or who are "too difficult" or "too different" from you? What truths could you inform yourself of that would make a true delight possible?

10. Is your highest desire to see others conformed to the image of Christ? What's your evidence? Could there be evidence that your highest desire is to see them act in ways which benefit you?

11. Are you excusing *any* area of sinfulness in your life that will always stunt your ability to love others well? What about areas of life that are not necessarily sinful but also hinder your ability to love?

12. What *specific* things are you sacrificing in order to love others well? What two things could you add to the list *this* week?

13. Do you have any subtle conditions as to whether you will love someone wholeheartedly? What are they? How can you do away with these?

14. Do you insist that others love you in ways that you get to define? What else do you think you may have imbibed from the culture as it pertains to love? Have you bought into any of the world's definitions of love? What are some Bible verses to combat these wrong ways of thinking?

15. Is your ultimate goal in life to bring glory to God by honoring and valuing Christ and finding your full satisfaction in Him? What else drives you? What other motivations do you find frequently popping up in your heart? Do you even analyze your heart? Your motives? Your thoughts and affections?

16. Do you help others look like Jesus? Do you make it easier or harder for them to sin by how you relate? List three people in your life and one habit you can start/stop for each to help them look more Christlike.

17. What do you mean when you say, "I love you," to someone? Does that line up with Scripture?

18. Is the quality and nature of your love personally—and your church's love corporately—such that people (believers and unbelievers) who encounter you are immediately impacted and enveloped in true love? How can you give off a sweet aroma of love this month? Name some larger, inward attitude changes and some smaller, outward, practical steps.

19. When the world looks at your church, what do they see? In what ways are you a blessing and/or a burden to your church?

20. In your own words (or mine), what's a comprehensive definition of love? Study it sufficiently to have it memorized. Review it daily.

Made in the USA
Middletown, DE
23 August 2024

59089959R00076